W9-BXY-286

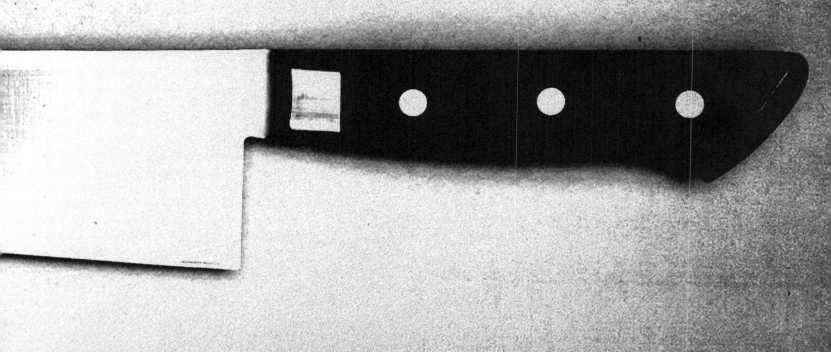

GARDE MANGER

CHUCK HUGHES

HarperCollins*Publishers*Ltd

Translated by Claudia M. Theriault

Garde-Manger
Original French language edition copyright © 2010 Les Éditions La Presse Ltée. All rights reserved.
English language translation copyright © 2012 HarperCollins Publishers Ltd. All rights reserved.

Originally published in French under the title "Garde-Manger" by Les Éditions La Presse Ltée, Montréal, Québec, Canada.

Published by HarperCollins Publishers Ltd, by arrangement with Les Éditions La Presse Ltée, Montréal, Québec, Canada.

First English-language edition

Photography
Dominique Lafond
www.dominiquelafond.com

Recipe writing and food styling
Johanne Depelteau

Kitchen Team
Chuck Hughes, Jean-François Méthot

Design and layout adapted from the original by Kuizin Studio
www.kuizin.com

No part of this book may be used or reproduced in any manner
whatsoever without the prior written permission of the publisher,
except in the case of brief quotations embodied in reviews.

HarperCollins books may be purchased for educational, business,
or sales promotional use through our Special Markets Department.

HarperCollins Publishers Ltd
2 Bloor Street East, 20th Floor
Toronto, Ontario, Canada
M4W 1A8

www.harpercollins.ca

Library and Archives Canada Cataloguing in Publication information is available upon request.

ISBN 978-1-44341-326-8

Printed and bound in Canada

TC 9 8 7 6 5 4 3 2 1

CHUCK HUGHES

FOR ANYONE WHO'S EVER COOKED ON
THE LINE OR WASHED DISHES

GARDE MANGER

TABLE DES MATIÈRES

INTRODUCTION

This book is a glimpse into the culinary universe of Garde-Manger, a "best of" our recipes, some standards, some tried-and-true classics, and some that I sincerely hope will inspire you. We are as passionate about cooking now as we were on our very first day. This book is our calling card, a sampling of our recipes at Garde-Manger, and above all a guide to our favourite dishes.

Writing a cookbook is no easy task. Food is constantly evolving, changing, becoming . . . Food is alive! Capturing something as ephemeral as a recipe or a favourite dish is anything but straightforward. Cuisine is guided by Mother Nature and her seasons, it is organic and follows its natural cycles. Actually, Mother Nature is the one who most often dictates what is on our menus!

Gathering the recipes presented in this book was a team effort. Jean-François Méthot and I chose our best-loved, our best-sellers, our own favourites along with a few new ones.

I would like to dedicate this book to my partners, Tim Rozon and Kyle Marshall-Nares, without whom there would be no Garde-Manger. Five years ago, all we had was a big dream and a little money, but with a lot of ingenuity and creativity, our "project" saw the light of day. As best friends, roommates, and business partners we shared the same vision, and decision making was always a team effort. Kyle's dedication and determination have been a major driving force behind our success. I am not sure we would be where we are without his perseverance. From renovations to accounting to picking wines, Kyle gets it all done, quietly and without fanfare. He has officially been nicknamed The Boss.

We built Garde-Manger together, one oyster at a time!

THANK YOU! CHUCK HUGHES

COCKTAILS

COCKTAILS

--

"A cocktail a day, every day" is a Garde-Manger mantra, so ours are always fun, festive, and epicurean. Every morning, the kitchen and bar crews put their heads together to come up with a cocktail du jour using only the freshest seasonal ingredients. Fresh fruit, fresh herbs, and more unusual ingredients like crab and lobster make an appearance.

BELLINI

Prep: 5 min -- Serves: 1

> ½ unpeeled peach
> 1 tbsp (15 mL) Chambord or other raspberry liqueur
> 1 drop orange bitters
> a few fresh raspberries
> Champagne or Prosecco

Mash the peach with a mortar and pestle. Put the mashed peach in a Champagne flute. Add the Chambord, orange bitters, and raspberries. Top up with Champagne. Stir gently.

NOTE
For a virgin version of this drink, use black currant or grenadine syrup with ginger ale.

CAMPARI WITH ORANGE SODA

Prep: 5 min -- Freezer time: 4 h -- Serves: 1

> **1 bottle Brio**
> **1½ oz (50 mL) Campari**
> **zest and juice of 1 orange**
> **seltzer (club soda)**

1. Pour the Brio into an ice cube tray and freeze.

2. Put a few Brio ice cubes in an Old-Fashioned glass. Pour the Campari and orange juice over them. Add the soda and orange zest, then give it a quick stir.

BLOODY CAESAR WITH CRAB LEGS

Prep: 5 min -- Serves: 1

This was our very first "drink of the day" at Garde-Manger. Tim Rozon, our "Michael Jordan of bartending," came up with the crab leg idea. It was an instant success and is now standard on our drinks menu.

> **lemon wedge**
> **steak spices (see recipe p. 101)**
> **2 oz (60 mL) vodka**
> **Clamato juice, to taste**
> **Tabasco sauce, to taste**
> **Worcestershire sauce, to taste**
> **couple of drops of lemon juice**
> **grated fresh horseradish**
> **slices of jalapeño peppers, to taste**
> **a celery rib and 1 or 2 crab legs, for garnish**

Use the lemon wedge to dampen the rim of a tall glass, then dip the rim in the steak spices. Over ice, pour the vodka, Clamato juice, Tabasco sauce, Worcestershire sauce, and lemon juice. Add horseradish and jalapeño slices. Garnish with a celery rib and crab legs.

GIN
WITH CUCUMBER AND DILL

Prep: 5 min -- Serves: 1

> **2 oz (60 mL) gin**
> **juice of ½ lime**
> **seltzer (club soda)**
> **2 sprigs dill, coarsely chopped, for garnish**
> **cucumber spear, for garnish**

Put some ice cubes in a highball glass and pour the gin and lime juice over them. Pour in the seltzer. Give it a quick stir. Garnish with the dill and the cucumber spear.

JACK DANIEL'S AND WATERMELON

Prep: 5 min -- Serves: 1

> **6 large cubes of watermelon**
> **2 oz (60 mL) Jack Daniel's**
> **sparkling water**
> **small sprig of basil, for garnish**

Put the watermelon and some ice cubes in a glass. Add the Jack Daniel's. Top it up with some sparkling water and stir. Garnish with the basil.

NOTE
You can also add a little sugar cane juice.

JOLLY RANCHER VODKA

Prep: 5 min -- Serves: 1

My partners, Kyle and Tim, and I worked together originally at Globe restaurant in Montreal. That experience ignited our passion for food and drink. Fifteen years ago, this was a popular drink all over town. It reminds us of our days starting out at Globe.

> **1 handful Jolly Rancher sour candies**
> **2 oz (60 mL) vodka**
> **orange slice, for garnish**

Put the candies and some ice cubes in an Old-Fashioned glass. Add the vodka. Give it a quick stir, then garnish with the orange slice.

VODKA WITH FRESH VANILLA AND CRUSHED STRAWBERRIES

Prep: 5 min -- Soaking time: 1 month -- Serves: 20

VANILLA VODKA
> 3 vanilla beans
> 1 bottle vodka

CRUSHED STRAWBERRIES
> ½ cup (125 mL) strawberries
> zest and juice of ½ lemon
> 1 tbsp (15 mL) sugar

GARNISH
> fresh strawberries
> vanilla bean, split lengthwise

For the vanilla vodka:
1. Split the vanilla beans in half lengthwise, scrape out the seeds, and put the beans and seeds into a full bottle of vodka. Cap it. Let steep in a cool, dark place for 1 month.

For the crushed strawberries:
2. Crush the strawberries with the lemon zest, lemon juice, and sugar.

3. In a shaker, put 2 oz (60 mL) of vanilla vodka, all the crushed strawberries, and a big handful of ice cubes. Shake well. Strain into a glass and garnish with fresh strawberries and a split vanilla bean.

STAFF MEALS

STAFF MEALS

--

The calm before the storm! After a full day of prep, we get together to take a break before diving into the night's work. It is the perfect moment to connect with each other and have a nosh. Staff meals are family meals at Garde-Manger, so conversation at the dinner table is friendly and relaxed.

Everyone at Garde-Manger settles down around the table between five and five thirty. When we have a little more time, members of the kitchen crew delight us with their own culinary creations. This is often when we sample new recipes and give our opinions! Sunday is always a special day, with all manner of seafood, scallops, and squid being served. A veritable feast.

33

BEEF BAVETTE (FLAP STEAK) AND FRITES

Prep: 15 min -- Refrigerate: 6 h -- Cook: 10 min -- Serves: 4

Garde-Manger was intended to be a seafood-only restaurant.
This was our one nod to the meat eaters on our first menu.
We've never been able to take it off! Simple is beautiful.

> **4 bavette (flap) steaks,
  each ½ lb (225 g)**
> **2 tbsp (30 mL) steak spices
  (see recipe p. 101)**
> **3 tbsp (45 mL) canola oil**
> **frites (see recipe p. 172)**
> **spicy mayonnaise
  (see recipe p. 111)**

MARINADE
> **¼ cup (60 mL) olive oil**
> **2 tbsp (30 mL) red wine vinegar**
> **1 garlic clove, finely chopped**
> **leaves from 2 sprigs rosemary,
  finely chopped**
> **leaves from 2 sprigs thyme,
  finely chopped**

SAUTÉED PEPPERS
> **12 miniature sweet peppers**
> **1 shallot, minced**
> **1 garlic clove, finely chopped**
> **salt and freshly ground pepper**

For the marinade:

1. In a large bowl, whisk together
   the olive oil, red wine vinegar,
   garlic, rosemary, and thyme.
   Add the steaks, turning them
   so they are well coated. Cover
   and refrigerate for 6 hours.

2. Drain the meat, discarding the
   marinade. Pat the steaks dry and
   coat on both sides with the steak
   spices. In a large cast-iron skillet,
   heat the canola oil on high. If you
   like your meat rare, cook the steaks
   for 4 minutes on one side, then
   flip them over and cook 2 minutes
   on the other side. Remove steaks
   from the pan and set aside.

For the peppers:

3. In the same pan over high heat,
   sauté the peppers with the shallots
   and the garlic until the peppers are
   soft. Season with salt and pepper.

4. Serve the steaks with the
   sautéed peppers, frites,
   and spicy mayonnaise.

NOTE
For a bavette to be tender, it should
be cooked rare, but not too rare.

Bavette leftovers are great with a
little soy sauce and steak spices.
Our staff and crew love it sautéed
with green onions and served with
pickles. I simply sauté big strips
of bavette in a sizzling-hot pan.

CALAMARI WITH PUTTANESCA SAUCE

Prep: 30 min -- Cook: 30 min -- Serves: 4

This simple, classic Italian sauce comes together quickly and packs a big punch. It's great with pasta, shrimp, or clams, too.

TOMATO BROTH
> 1 tbsp (15 mL) olive oil
> 1 shallot, minced
> 8 Roma tomatoes, cut in half lengthwise
> 1 cup (250 mL) water
> 5 big handfuls basil leaves
> 1 sprig rosemary
> rind of leftover piece of Parmesan
> salt and freshly ground pepper

CALAMARI WITH PUTTANESCA SAUCE
> 2 tbsp (30 mL) olive oil
> ½ head roasted garlic (see recipe p. 96)
> 1 anchovy fillet
> 1 lb (450 g) peeled and sliced calamari
> 20 pitted Kalamata olives
> 2 tbsp (30 mL) capers
> 1 handful chopped basil
> 1 handful chopped parsley
> 1 handful chopped celery leaves
> salt and freshly ground pepper

GARNISHES
> 8 large steak spice croutons (see recipe p. 100), about 3 inches (8 cm) each
> olive oil
> zest of 1 lemon
> chopped parsley

For the tomato broth:

1. In a large saucepan, heat the oil over medium-low and sweat the shallot until softened. Using your hands, press the tomatoes to extract the juices (discard the juices), then add the squeezed tomato halves to the pan. Add the water, basil, rosemary, and Parmesan rind; simmer for 15 minutes. Strain the broth through a sieve, pressing on the solids to extract the maximum amount of liquid; discard the solids. Season the broth with salt and pepper. Set aside.

For the calamari:

2. Heat the oil in a large skillet over medium-high. Squeeze the garlic pulp from the skins and add to the pan with the anchovy; mash them with a wooden spoon. Stir in the calamari and sauté for 2 minutes. Add the olives, capers, and reserved tomato broth. Simmer for 2 minutes. Stir in the basil, parsley, and celery leaves. Season with salt and pepper. Remove from heat.

3. Place a large crouton on each plate. Spoon some of the calamari and puttanesca over top. Finish with a second crouton. Drizzle with a bit of olive oil and garnish with lemon zest and parsley.

CHIPOTLE PORK CHOPS WITH POTATO RISOTTO

Prep: 30 min -- Cook: 30 min -- Serves: 4

You have to try making potato risotto. Cooked risotto-style, the potatoes become incredibly creamy and tender. And how can you go wrong with potatoes, Parmesan, and cream?

PORK CHOPS
> 1 can (198 g) chipotle peppers in adobo sauce
> 4 pork chops, each 2 inches (5 cm) thick
> salt and freshly ground pepper
> 3 tbsp (45 mL) olive oil
> chopped parsley, for garnish

POTATO RISOTTO
> 4 Yukon Gold potatoes, diced
> 2 tbsp (30 mL) butter
> ½ cup (125 mL) 35% cream
> ½ cup (125 mL) grated Parmigiano-Reggiano
> ¼ cup (60 mL) finely chopped chives
> salt and freshly ground pepper

WHITE VERMOUTH SAUCE
> 2 cups (500 mL) dry vermouth
> 1 shallot, minced
> 1 cup (250 mL) veal stock (see recipe p. 106)
> 1 tbsp (15 mL) butter
> salt and freshly ground pepper

For the pork chops:
1. In a blender, purée the chipotle peppers with their sauce. Season the chops with salt and pepper. Generously brush the chops on both sides with the puréed chipotles.

For the potato risotto:
2. Cook the potatoes in a pot of boiling salted water until they are just tender, about 8 minutes. Drain. In a large saucepan, bring 1 cup (250 mL) water to a boil over medium-high heat. Whisk in the butter. Add the diced potatoes. Using a wooden spoon, stir the potatoes gently for a couple of minutes. Turn down the heat to medium and drizzle in the cream, a spoonful at a time, waiting until it's nearly absorbed before adding the next spoonful. Keep stirring until the potatoes are creamy but still have a bit of texture. There should be some lumps. Add the Parmesan and chives; mix well. Season with salt and pepper. Remove from heat and keep warm.

3. Preheat the oven to 450°F (230°C).

4. Heat the olive oil in a large cast-iron skillet on high heat. Cook the pork chops until browned on the bottom. Turn the chops, transfer them to the oven, and continue cooking for 7 minutes. Remove the pan from the oven, cover with foil, and let rest for 10 minutes. The chops will continue cooking from the residual heat, going from rare to well done.

For the white vermouth sauce:
5. Remove the chops from the pan and keep warm. Drain the fat from the pan. Deglaze with the dry vermouth, then flambé. When the flames die out, add the shallot and cook, stirring, until the pan is almost dry. Add the veal stock. Simmer for a few minutes, then swirl in the butter. Season with salt and pepper.

6. Serve the chops with the potato risotto and green beans sautéed in butter with shallots. Spoon the sauce over the chops and potatoes. Garnish with parsley.

VEAL CHEEKS IN BEER

Prep: 15 min -- Cook: 3 h 30 -- Serves: 4

This is just one of those comforting, easy recipes, perfect for a cold Montreal winter evening. Talk to your butcher; he'll be able to find you great veal cheeks.

> 2 lb (900 g) veal cheeks
>   (8 cheeks)
> salt and freshly ground pepper
> 3 tbsp (45 mL) canola oil
> ½ lb (225 g) bacon, diced
> 1 onion, chopped
> leaves from 4 sprigs thyme,
>   chopped
> 5 cups (1.25 L) Bierbrier beer
>   or your favourite lager
> 1 cup (250 mL) veal stock
>   (see recipe p. 106)
> ¼ cup (60 mL) butter, cubed

SIDE DISHES
> celeriac rémoulade
>   (see recipe p. 119)
> relish

1. Preheat the oven to 350°F (180°C).

2. Season the veal cheeks with salt and pepper. In a large ovenproof pan such as a Dutch oven, heat the oil over medium-high. Brown the meat on all sides. Remove the meat from the pan. Add the bacon and cook for a couple of minutes. Add the onion and cook until transparent. Stir in the thyme. Put the meat back in the pan. Add the beer. Cover the pan, put it in the oven, and braise the veal for about 3 hours or until the meat is tender enough to cut with a fork. Remove the veal from the pan and keep warm.

3. Set a sieve over a medium saucepan and strain the cooking liquid into the pot. Reserve the solids for the garnish. Skim the fat off the surface with a ladle. Add the veal stock. Bring to a boil, then simmer until the sauce is reduced by half or until it is thick enough to coat a spoon. Whisk in the butter a cube at a time. Adjust the seasoning.

4. Lay 2 veal cheeks on a bed of celeriac rémoulade. Garnish with the bacon and onion, a ladleful of sauce, and some relish.

DE L'OMOPLATE

OMOPLATE

OS DU BILLON

OS DU COU

I ♥ KYLE ATLAS

OS DE LA

BRÉCHET

OS DE LA JOINTURE
DU JARRET

OS DU JARRET
DE DEVANT

41

FRIED STUFFED POBLANO CHILIES

Prep: 30 min -- Cook: 15 min -- Serves: 4

I call this the restaurant's version of your mom's tuna casserole: for us, it's a "store cupboard" recipe. We always have the ingredients lying around, and the staff is always thrilled when we make it for the staff meal.

BLUE CHEESE SAUCE
> 1 cup (250 mL) 35% cream
> 1 cup (250 mL) crumbled blue cheese
> freshly ground pepper

STUFFED POBLANO CHILIES
> 8 poblano chilies
> 2 tbsp (30 mL) olive oil
> 1 large onion, minced
> 1 lb (450 g) ground beef
> 2 hot Italian sausages, casings removed
> ½ cup (125 mL) veal stock (see recipe p. 106)
> leaves from 6 sprigs thyme, chopped
> salt and freshly ground pepper
> ½ cup (125 mL) diced mozzarella cheese
> ½ cup (125 mL) diced aged Cheddar cheese
> ½ cup (125 mL) diced Monterey Jack cheese
> canola or peanut oil for deep-frying
> 1 cup (250 mL) flour
> 1¼ cups (300 mL) pale ale

GARNISHES
> chopped parsley
> chopped chives
> grated Parmigiano-Reggiano
> grape must or aged balsamic vinegar

For the blue cheese sauce:
1. In a small saucepan over medium heat, heat the cream. Add the blue cheese and stir until melted. Season with pepper. Remove from heat and keep warm.

For the stuffed poblano chilies:
2. In a large skillet on high heat, brown the poblano chilies on all sides in half of the oil. Remove them from the pan and let cool.

3. In the same skillet, heat the remaining olive oil over medium-high heat. Sweat the onions until softened but not colouring. Add the ground beef and the sausage meat; cook for several minutes, breaking up the meat with a wooden spoon, until the meat is no longer pink. Add the veal stock and thyme; cook for a few minutes to pull the flavours together. Season with salt and pepper. Let cool. Stir in the mozzarella, Cheddar, and Monterey Jack.

4. Cut the chilies in half lengthwise, without severing the two halves, and remove the seeds. Stuff the chilies with the meat mixture and press both sides back together.

5. Heat the canola oil in a deep-fryer or large, deep pot to 350°F (180°C).

6. In a bowl, mix the flour with salt and pepper. Whisk in enough ale to make a batter the consistency of thick cream.

7. Dip the stuffed chilies into the batter. Fry them in the hot oil, turning them occasionally, for 2 minutes or until pale golden. Drain on paper towels and season with salt and pepper.

8. Arrange the chilies on a platter or individual plates. Pour the blue cheese sauce over them. Garnish with parsley, chives, Parmesan, and a few drops of grape must to taste.

NOTE
You can use many different cheeses in the stuffing. Try it with smoked gouda, for example.

CHORIZO AND MAMIROLLE RACLETTE

Prep: 30 min -- Cook: 15 min -- Serves: 4

This is our version of a wintry Québécois favourite.
The cured chorizo gives an intense flavour hit.

> 2 sweet red peppers, cut in half lengthwise, seeds removed
> 2 tbsp (30 mL) olive oil
> salt and freshly ground pepper
> 2 lb (900 g) cured chorizo, cut in ½-inch (1 cm) slices
> 12 cooked fingerling potatoes, cut in half lengthwise
> 8 cipollini onions, peeled and cut in half lengthwise
> 8 slices Le Mamirolle, Gruyère, or any good melting cheese
> 4 green onions, thinly sliced

1. Preheat the broiler.

2. Place the peppers, skin side up, on a small baking sheet. Drizzle with half of the olive oil and sprinkle with salt and pepper. Broil the peppers until the skin is blackened. Put the peppers in a bowl, cover, and let sit for 30 minutes. Peel off the skins and cut the peppers into strips.

3. Preheat the broiler again.

4. In a large cast-iron skillet over medium-high, sauté the chorizo in the remaining olive oil until browned. Add the fingerling potatoes and the onions; cook until the potatoes are browned on all sides. Stir in the broiled peppers. Top with slices of Mamirolle and broil until the cheese is golden brown.

5. Garnish with the green onions and serve with toast.

NOTE
You can also blacken the pepper skins by putting them directly over a gas burner or on a barbecue.

OCTOPUS SALAD WITH FENNEL, GREEN APPLES, AND PISTACHIOS

Prep: 15 min -- Cook: 1 h 30 -- Serves: 4

This salad reappears on our menu every summer because our patrons love it so much. It's crisp, light, and unusual.

- > 1½ lb (675 g) squid, cleaned
- > 1 fennel bulb, cut in quarters lengthwise
- > 2 lemons (halved)
- > 1 cup (250 mL) fennel salad (see recipe p. 118)
- > 2 julienned green apples
- > 4 cups (1 L) arugula
- > ¼ cup (60 mL) salted roasted pistachios
- > 1 handful chopped parsley
- > 1 handful chopped chives
- > salt and freshly ground pepper

1. To a large pot of boiling salted water, add the squid and the fennel quarters. Squeeze the juice of the lemons into the pot and then add the lemon halves. Simmer for 1½ hours or until the squid is very tender.

2. Drain the squid and let it cool. Cut off the tentacles, discarding the remaining squid. Skin the tentacles, leaving the suction cups intact in order to expose the nice white flesh. Cut the tentacles into ½-inch (1 cm) slices.

3. Toss together the squid, fennel salad, apples, arugula, pistachios, parsley, and chives. Season with salt and pepper. Arrange on plates and serve.

NOTE

The squid will actually be cooked after 15 minutes, but continuing to cook it for the whole 1½ hours will make it very tender (just like chicken). Do not overcook it, though, as the flesh would turn to mush.

LAMB STEAKS WITH CARAMELIZED FINGERLING POTATOES

Prep: 15 min -- Cook: 45 min -- Serves: 4

We get the butcher to cut a whole leg of lamb into steaks, similar to osso buco. This is an absolute winner, easy and incredibly tasty.

CARAMELIZED FINGERLING POTATOES
> 1 lb (450 g) fingerling potatoes, cut in half lengthwise
> leaves from 2 sprigs thyme, chopped
> leaves from 2 sprigs rosemary, chopped
> 1 garlic clove, minced
> 3 tbsp (45 mL) olive oil
> salt and freshly ground pepper

LAMB STEAKS
> 4 thick crosswise slices leg of lamb, with bone
> 3 tbsp (45 mL) olive oil
> Maldon sea salt
> coarsely ground pepper

1. Preheat the oven to 350°F (180°C).

For the fingerling potatoes:

2. Combine the potatoes with the thyme, rosemary, garlic, olive oil, and salt and pepper. Toss to coat the fingerlings. Place the potatoes, cut side down, on a baking sheet. Roast for 45 minutes or until tender and caramelized. Keep warm.

For the lamb steaks:

3. When the potatoes are nearly done, heat a large cast-iron skillet over high heat. Coat the lamb steaks with the olive oil, then season them with salt and pepper. Cook the steaks, turning once, for 3 to 4 minutes per side if you like your lamb rare.

4. Serve the lamb steaks with the caramelized fingerling potatoes.

SARDINES AND ROASTED TOMATOES ON TOAST

Prep: 30 min -- Cook: 15 min -- Serves: 4

These roasted tomatoes brighten up so many dishes. We always have them on hand at the restaurant. Use them as a simple sauce for pasta or stir them into a stew.

ROASTED TOMATOES
> 2 tbsp (30 mL) olive oil
> 1 fennel bulb, thinly sliced
> 8 cipollini onions, quartered
> 12 cherry tomatoes, cut in half
> salt and freshly ground pepper
> 1 bunch chives, finely chopped
> 1 bunch dill, finely chopped
> 1 bunch baby basil leaves
> 1 tsp (5 mL) white balsamic vinegar

GRILLED TOAST
> 2 tbsp (30 mL) olive oil
> 4 slices country loaf
> ¼ cup (60 mL) seasoned sour cream (see recipe p. 98)

CAVIAR VINAIGRETTE
> 1 tbsp (15 mL) trout caviar (roe)
> 1 tbsp (15 mL) olive oil
> 1 tsp (5 mL) white balsamic vinegar
> 1 handful chopped chives
> 1 handful chopped parsley

SARDINES
> salt and freshly ground pepper
> 4 large fresh sardines, gutted and filleted
> 2 tbsp (30 mL) canola oil

For the roasted tomatoes:
1. Heat half of the olive oil in a large skillet over medium-high heat. Cook the fennel, onions, and tomatoes just a few minutes, stirring frequently, until tender. Season with salt and pepper. Transfer to a bowl. Stir in the chives, dill, basil, white balsamic vinegar, and the remaining olive oil.

For the grilled toast:
2. Wipe out the skillet, and heat the olive oil on medium-high. Add the bread and toast it until golden. Remove from the pan and set aside.

For the vinaigrette:
3. Combine all the ingredients. Mix well. Keep in the fridge if you're not using it right away.

For the sardines:
4. Salt and pepper the sardines. Heat the canola oil in a cast-iron skillet over medium-high heat. Cook the sardines, skin side down, for 1 minute, pressing lightly with a spatula so they cook evenly.

5. Spread the seasoned sour cream on the toast. Top with a spoonful of the roasted tomatoes. Place a couple of sardine fillets on top and drizzle with a spoonful of the caviar vinaigrette.

NOTE
You can ask your fishmonger to gut and fillet the sardines.

You can also poach the sardines in olive oil and vegetables (a dish known as escabèche).

You can use different herbs, whatever your taste.

We had no country loaf when taking the picture, so we used sliced white bread!

During this photo shoot, our lunch consisted of leftover roasted tomatoes and leftover tomato and avocado salad. Once mixed, we had a totally different dish!

51

AMAAAZING!

53

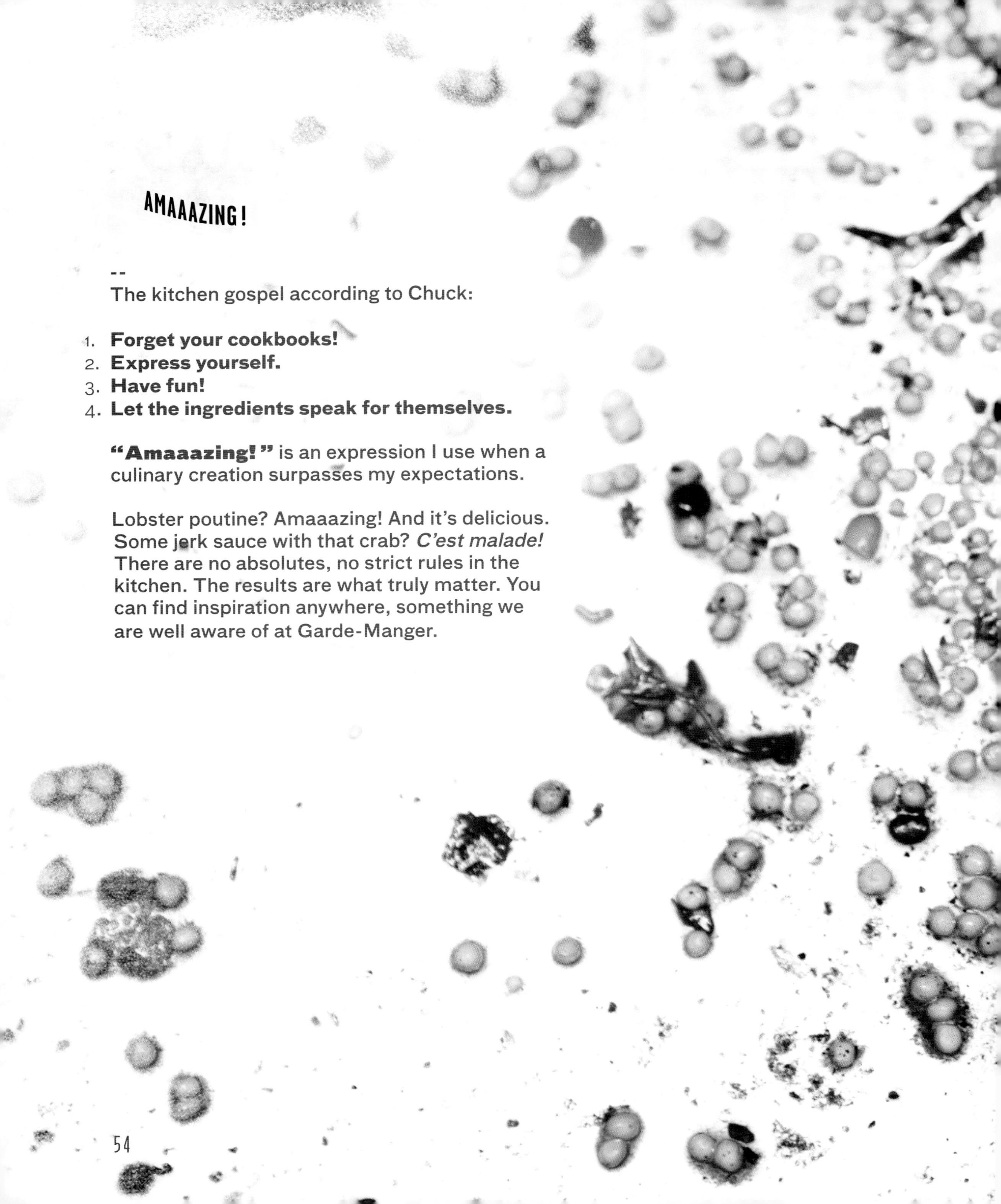

AMAAAZING !

--

The kitchen gospel according to Chuck:

1. **Forget your cookbooks!**
2. **Express yourself.**
3. **Have fun!**
4. **Let the ingredients speak for themselves.**

"Amaaazing!" is an expression I use when a culinary creation surpasses my expectations.

Lobster poutine? Amaaazing! And it's delicious. Some jerk sauce with that crab? *C'est malade!* There are no absolutes, no strict rules in the kitchen. The results are what truly matter. You can find inspiration anywhere, something we are well aware of at Garde-Manger.

CLAMS AND FRIED PEROGIES

Prep: 15 min -- Cook: 10 min -- Serves: 4

Crazy combination, right? This dish came out of our love of the perogies from Stash Café, the Polish restaurant down the street. Somehow someone ate one with some leftover clams and a genius dish was born. These fried perogies are incredibly crispy and creamy.

FRIED PEROGIES
> canola or peanut oil for deep-frying
> 20 perogies (see recipe p. 107)
> salt

CLAMS
> 4 cups (1L) water
> 2 tbsp (30 mL) butter
> 2 lb (900 g) clams, cleaned
> 1 handful chopped dill
> 1 handful chopped parsley
> 1 handful finely chopped chives
> freshly ground pepper

GARNISHES
> 4 slices bacon, cubed and cooked
> 1 green onion, finely chopped
> ¼ cup (60 mL) seasoned sour cream (see recipe p. 98)

For the fried perogies:
1. Heat the oil in a deep-fryer or large, deep pot to 350°F (180°C).

2. Fry the perogies for just a couple of minutes, until they are golden and crispy. Drain on paper towels and season with salt.

For the clams:
3. In a large pot, bring the water and the butter to a boil. Add the clams and cook until they open. Using a slotted spoon, transfer the clams to a bowl. Toss them with the dill, parsley, chives, and pepper.

4. Spoon the fried perogies onto plates. Follow with the clams. Garnish with the bacon, green onion, and seasoned sour cream. Finish with a dash of freshly ground pepper.

NOTE
I prefer the clams poached and the perogies fried—they have more texture that way. But you can also fry the clams and poach the perogies. It's all a matter of taste.

Poach the perogies in the same mixture of water and butter for 3 to 4 minutes.

To fry the clams, remove them from their shells and dredge them in a mixture of flour and cornmeal. Beat an egg, coat the clams with the egg, and dredge them once again in the flour mixture. Fry them in the hot oil until golden.

ARANCINI AND LOBSTER BISQUE

Prep: 30 min -- Cook: 15 min -- Serves: 4

We make a lot of risotto at the restaurant, and when there's leftovers, arancini (risotto balls) are a go-to dish for us. They are insanely good with the deeply flavourful lobster bisque. The risotto I've used here is our rock shrimp risotto without the mushroom garnish, but of course you can use whatever leftover risotto you have.

CRAB GARNISH

> 2 cups (500 mL) shredded crab meat (about 4 handfuls)
> 2 tbsp (30 mL) finely chopped chives
> celery leaves, to taste
> zest of 1 lemon
> salt and freshly ground pepper

LOBSTER BISQUE

> 2 tbsp (30 mL) butter
> 2 tbsp (30 mL) flour
> 4 cups (1 L) lobster stock (see recipe p. 105), reduced by half
> salt and freshly ground pepper

ARANCINI (RISOTTO BALLS)

> canola or peanut oil for deep-frying
> 3 cups (750 mL) risotto (see recipe p. 84)
> ½ cup (125 mL) grated Parmigiano-Reggiano
> 1 cup (250 mL) flour
> salt and freshly ground pepper
> 4 eggs
> 1 cup (250 mL) panko bread crumbs

For the crab garnish:
1. Combine all the garnish ingredients. Keep cool in the refrigerator.

For the lobster bisque:
2. In a large pot, melt the butter over medium heat. Add the flour and cook, stirring constantly, for 2 minutes. Whisk in the lobster stock and cook another 10 minutes, stirring occasionally, until lightly thickened and no floury taste remains. Season with salt and pepper. Set aside and keep warm.

For the arancini:
3. Preheat the oil in a deep-fryer or large, deep pot to 350°F (180°C).

4. In a bowl, mix the risotto and Parmesan. Shape into 2-inch (5 cm) balls.

5. In another bowl, season the flour with salt and pepper. In a third bowl, beat the eggs. Pour the panko crumbs into a fourth bowl. Coat each risotto ball with the flour, roll in the beaten eggs, then dredge in the panko.

6. Fry the arancini in the hot oil until crispy and golden, about 4 to 5 minutes.

7. Serve the arancini in a pool of the lobster bisque and garnish with the crab mixture.

GOAT CHEESE AND LENTIL BRUSCHETTA

Prep: 30 min -- Cook: 30 to 45 min -- Serves: 4

Okay, it's not your average bruschetta, but let's be honest—anything with goat cheese sells! And this dish is seriously savoury, creamy, saucy, and good.

LENTILS
> 2 cups (500 mL) Puy or beluga lentils
> 1 carrot, coarsely chopped
> 1 celery rib, coarsely chopped
> 1 onion, quartered
> ¼ lb (115 g) bacon
> salt and freshly ground pepper

RED WINE SAUCE
> 2 cups (500 mL) veal stock (see recipe p. 106 or use store-bought)
> 2 cups (500 mL) red wine
> ¼ cup (60 mL) brown sugar
> 2 tbsp (30 mL) butter, diced
> salt and freshly ground pepper

GOAT CHEESE CROUTONS
> 2 tbsp (30 mL) olive oil
> 4 thick slices country loaf
> 4 cloves roasted garlic (see recipe p. 96)
> 1 cup (250 mL) fresh goat cheese
> salt and freshly ground pepper

CRISPY PANCETTA
> 8 thin slices pancetta

TOMATOES POACHED IN OLIVE OIL
> 1½ cups (375 mL) olive oil
> 12 cherry tomatoes

SWISS CHARD
> 1 tbsp (15 mL) butter
> 4 large leaves Swiss chard, blanched and coarsely chopped
> Maldon sea salt and freshly ground pepper
> grape must

For the lentils:

1. In a pot of boiling salted water, place the lentils, carrot, celery, onion, and bacon. Turn the heat down to a simmer and cook for about 30 minutes, until the lentils are tender. Drain the lentils, and discard the vegetables and bacon. Set aside the lentils and keep warm.

For the red wine sauce:

2. Meanwhile, in a saucepan, simmer the veal stock with the red wine and brown sugar for about 30 to 45 minutes, until the sauce thickens and is reduced by half. Whisk in the butter, one cube at a time. Season with salt and pepper. Set aside and keep warm.

For the goat cheese croutons:

3. Heat the oil in a large skillet over medium-high heat. Add the bread and toast it until golden. Spread the roasted garlic on the toasts. Set aside.

For the crispy pancetta:

4. Preheat the oven to 350°F (180°C).

5. Place the slices of pancetta on a baking sheet lined with parchment paper. Cover with a second sheet of parchment paper and another baking sheet to ensure the pancetta stays nice and flat. Bake for 15 minutes or until the pancetta is crispy.

For the tomatoes:

6. Pour the olive oil into a small saucepan and heat on medium. When the oil is hot, add the tomatoes. When the tomato skins begin to split (after about 3 minutes), strain the tomatoes and set aside. (Reserve the oil for another use.)

For the Swiss chard:

7. In a medium saucepan, melt the butter over medium-high heat and sauté the Swiss chard. Add the lentils and season with salt and pepper.

8. Spread most of the goat cheese on the croutons. Put a small dollop of goat cheese in the middle of each plate so the croutons won't slip. Put the croutons on the plates and top with the pancetta. Spoon on the lentils and poached tomatoes. Pour the sauce on top. Season with Maldon salt and pepper. Drizzle with the grape must.

NOTE
Beluga lentils are smaller and much darker than Puy lentils. You can use either kind in this recipe.

CHICHARRONES

Prep: 5 min -- Cook: 1 to 2 min -- Serves: 4

Is there anything more dangerously delicious than crispy, fried pork belly? Addictive!

> canola or peanut oil for deep-frying
> 4 slices preserved pork belly
> ½ cup (125 mL) seasoned sour cream (see recipe p. 98)
> watercress or salad greens

1. Heat the oil in a deep-fryer or large, deep pot to 350°F (180°C).

2. Fry the slices of pork belly for about a minute, until golden and crispy. Serve with the seasoned sour cream and the cress.

PRESERVED PORK BELLY

Prep: 10 min -- Marinate: 4 h -- Cook: 4 h -- Serves: 6 to 8

> 4 lb (1.8 kg) pork belly
> coarse sea salt
> 1 tsp (5 mL) black peppercorns
> 6 sprigs rosemary
> 6 sprigs thyme
> 1 head garlic, cut in half crosswise
> 12 cups (3 L) duck fat, melted

1. In a nonreactive dish, place the meat on a bed of coarse sea salt. Cover with a mixture of more salt, the pepper, rosemary, thyme, and garlic. Let sit in the fridge for 4 hours.

2. Preheat the oven to 325°F (160°C).

3. Rinse the meat, dry it off, and put it in a baking dish. Cover it with the duck fat. Cook in the oven for 3 to 4 hours, until the meat is fork-tender. Let cool in the fat. The preserved pork belly can be stored, refrigerated in the fat, for several weeks. Before using, remove from the fat. (Freeze the fat to use again.)

NOTE

The best cut of pork belly is the centre cut. That is where you'll find the best fat-to-meat ratio.

To make confit or preserve, use this technique for chicken legs, turkey legs, duck legs, guinea hen legs, rabbit, and so on. The cooking time will differ, but what you want is for your meat to be luscious and fork-tender.

LAUGHING BIRD SHRIMP IN BÉCHAMEL SAUCE WITH FRESH BABY PEAS

Prep: 15 min -- Cook: 10 min -- Serves: 4

Laughing Bird shrimp come from Belize. Highly sustainable, fresh, and never frozen, they are sweet and delicious, and we can never keep enough on hand.

BÉCHAMEL SAUCE

> 1 cup (250 mL) grated 2-year-old Île-aux-Grues or other white Cheddar cheese
> 1 cup (250 mL) grated mild orange Cheddar cheese
> ¼ cup (60 mL) butter
> ¼ cup (60 mL) flour
> 4 cups (1 L) milk
> salt and freshly ground pepper

SHRIMP

> 1 lb (450 g) Laughing Bird shrimp
> 1 tbsp (15 mL) canola oil
> 2 tbsp (30 mL) butter
> 1 shallot, thinly sliced
> ½ lb (225 g) fresh baby peas, shelled
> salt and freshly ground pepper

For the béchamel:

1. Toss together the white and orange Cheddars. In a medium saucepan on medium heat, melt the butter. Add the flour and cook, stirring constantly, for 2 minutes. Whisk in the milk and bring to a boil. Reduce heat and simmer, stirring until the sauce thickens. Add half the cheese and stir until it has melted. Season with salt and pepper. Set aside.

For the shrimp:

2. Preheat the broiler.

3. In a large ovenproof skillet on high heat, sauté the shrimp in the oil until they just turn pink, then stir in the butter, shallot, and peas.

4. Divide the mixture evenly among ovenproof plates. Top with the béchamel sauce and sprinkle with the remaining cheese. Broil until the cheese is bubbling and turning golden brown. Serve immediately.

NOTE

Laughing Bird shrimp, which you can find at any good fishmonger, are small and sweet. They have no iodine taste, as they are organically farmed. If they are too hard to find, any other type of shrimp will do.

At our restaurant we make béchamel in large quantities ahead of time, so this particular dish is quick and easy. At home, you can store béchamel sauce in the fridge for up to a week.

ROAST HALIBUT WITH CARROT BUTTER

Prep: 30 min -- Cook: 30 min -- Serves: 4

The carrot butter in this dish is good on any roasted white fish, but at the restaurant we most often pair it with simply seared scallops. It will keep in the fridge, covered, for about a week.

NANTES CARROTS
> 2 slices bacon, diced
> 1 lb (450 g) Nantes or other sweet new carrots, chopped roughly if large
> ¼ cup (60 mL) butter, softened
> salt and freshly ground pepper

PEROGIES
> 8 perogies (see recipe p. 107)
> 1 tbsp (15 mL) butter
> salt and freshly ground pepper

GREEN BEANS
> 2 tbsp (30 mL) butter
> 1 shallot, finely chopped
> ½ lb (225 g) green beans, cut in half lengthwise
> salt and freshly ground pepper

HALIBUT
> 1 tbsp (15 mL) canola oil
> 4 thick skin-on halibut fillets
> salt and freshly ground pepper
--
> 1 cup (250 mL) carrot butter (see recipe p. 96)

For the Nantes carrots:
1. Cook the bacon until crispy. Drain on paper towels.

2. Meanwhile, boil the carrots in salted water until tender, then drain. Mash the carrots with the butter until almost puréed. Stir in the bacon. Season with salt and pepper. Set aside and keep warm.

For the perogies:
3. In a pot of boiling salted water, cook the perogies for 2 to 3 minutes or until cooked through. Drain. In a large skillet over medium-high heat, melt the butter, then sauté the perogies until lightly coloured. Season with salt and pepper. Set aside and keep warm.

For the green beans:
4. In another large skillet over medium-high heat, melt the butter. Sauté the shallot and the green beans just until the beans are cooked. Season with salt and pepper. Set aside and keep warm.

For the halibut:
5. Preheat the oven to 400°F (200°C).

6. Heat the oil in a large ovenproof skillet over high heat. Cook the halibut, skin side down, until the skin is golden and crispy, about 2 minutes. Turn the fish over, transfer the pan to the oven, and continue cooking for 8 minutes.

7. Spoon the mashed carrots and the green beans onto individual plates. Add 2 perogies and a piece of halibut. Top with some of the carrot butter.

FRIED HOT CHICKEN ON WAFFLES

Prep: 30 min -- Cook: 1 h -- Serves: 4

This truly is phenomenal: deep-fried confit chicken with waffles and gorgeous gravy. Go crazy!

GRAVY
> 4 cups (1 L) chicken stock (see recipe p. 104)
> 2 cups (500 mL) white wine
> 1 tbsp (15 mL) cornstarch, dissolved in a bit of water
> salt and freshly ground pepper
> 2 tbsp (30 mL) Dijon mustard
> 1 cup (250 mL) butter, diced

FRIED PRESERVED DRUMSTICKS
> canola or peanut oil for deep-frying
> 1 cup (250 mL) flour
> 1 tsp (5 mL) cayenne pepper
> 1 tsp (5 mL) smoked hot paprika
> 4 eggs
> 8 preserved chicken drumsticks (see preserved pork belly recipe p. 62)

GARNISH
> 2 cups (500 mL) baby peas
> ½ lb (225 g) chanterelles or other mushrooms, roughly chopped
> 3 tbsp (45 mL) butter
> salt and freshly ground pepper
--
> 4 waffles (see recipe p. 110)

For the gravy:
1. In a large saucepan, reduce the chicken stock to 1 cup (250 mL). At the same time, in another saucepan, reduce the white wine to ½ cup (125 mL).

2. Add the reduced wine to the stock. Bring to a simmer. Give the cornstarch mixture a stir, then whisk it into the stock. Season with salt and pepper.

3. Whisk in the mustard. Reduce heat and whisk in the butter, one piece at a time.

4. Remove from heat and set aside.

For the fried preserved drumsticks:
5. Heat the oil in a deep-fryer or large, deep pot to 350°F (180°C).

6. In a bowl, mix the flour with the cayenne and paprika. In a second bowl, beat the eggs. Dredge the drumsticks in the flour mixture, then in the beaten eggs, and once again in the flour mixture.

7. Fry for a couple of minutes or until the drumsticks are golden and crispy. Drain on paper towels.

For the garnish:
8. In a large skillet over medium-high heat, sauté the peas and the mushrooms in the butter until the mushrooms are becoming golden and peas are cooked through. Add 3 big ladles of gravy. Season with salt and pepper.

9. Place a waffle on each plate. Spoon the mushrooms and peas over the waffles. Top with the fried drumsticks. If you like, serve with frites (see recipe p. 172).

SPICY LOBSTER, CREAMED CORN, AND WATERCRESS WITH SMOKED TOMATO VINAIGRETTE

Prep: 30 min -- Cook: 1 h -- Serves: 4

CREAMED CORN

> 2 cups (500 mL) 35% cream
> ½ head roasted garlic (see recipe p. 96)
> kernels from 12 cobs of corn
> 2 tbsp (30 mL) butter
> salt and freshly ground pepper
> ¼ cup (60 mL) grated Parmigiano-Reggiano
> 1 bunch chives, finely chopped

SPICY LOBSTER

> 2 leeks (white part only), finely chopped
> 1 stalk lemongrass, finely chopped
> 1 inch (2.5 cm) fresh ginger, peeled and finely chopped
> 1 garlic clove, finely chopped
> 4 jalapeño peppers, seeded and sliced
> 2 green onions, finely chopped
> 4 kaffir lime leaves, torn in half
> 4 fresh bay leaves, torn in half
> 4 lobsters, each 1½ lb (675 g) or bigger if you like
> ¼ cup (60 mL) butter
> 2 cups (500 mL) smoked tomato vinaigrette (see recipe p. 135)
> chopped parsley and chives, for garnish

For the creamed corn:

1. Pour the cream into a large skillet. Squeeze the garlic pulp into the cream. Bring to a boil. Reduce heat to low, add the corn, and simmer for 1 hour, until the corn mixture is thick, creamy, and irresistible. Stir in the butter. Season with salt and pepper. Set aside and keep warm.

For the spicy lobster:

2. Preheat the oven to 450°F (230°C).

3. In a bowl, combine the leeks, lemongrass, ginger, garlic, jalapeño, green onions, lime leaves, and bay leaves. Set aside.

4. In a large pot of boiling salted water, cook the lobsters for 1½ to 2 minutes. Cool in chilled water. Cut in half lengthwise and clean. Crack the claws.

5. In a large cast-iron skillet over high heat, bring 1 cup (250 mL) water and the butter to a boil. Put the lobsters in the pan, shell side down. Top with the vegetable and herb mixture. Pour the smoked tomato vinaigrette over top. Put the pan in the oven and roast for 5 minutes or until the lobster is just done.

6. Serve the lobsters garnished with the parsley and chives. Serve the creamed corn as a side dish with the grated Parmesan and chopped chives on top.

NOTE

People tend to overcook lobster. If you buy fresh live lobster, you can actually eat it cooked rare just like a steak.

Roasting the lobster shell side down prevents it from drying out and renders juicier lobster meat.

The tail meat is usually slightly transparent when the lobster is done.

At the restaurant we usually present this dish with a radicchio and watercress salad. Depending on the season, you can use endive instead of radicchio, and lamb's lettuce or arugula instead of watercress. Of course, you don't have to serve it with greens!

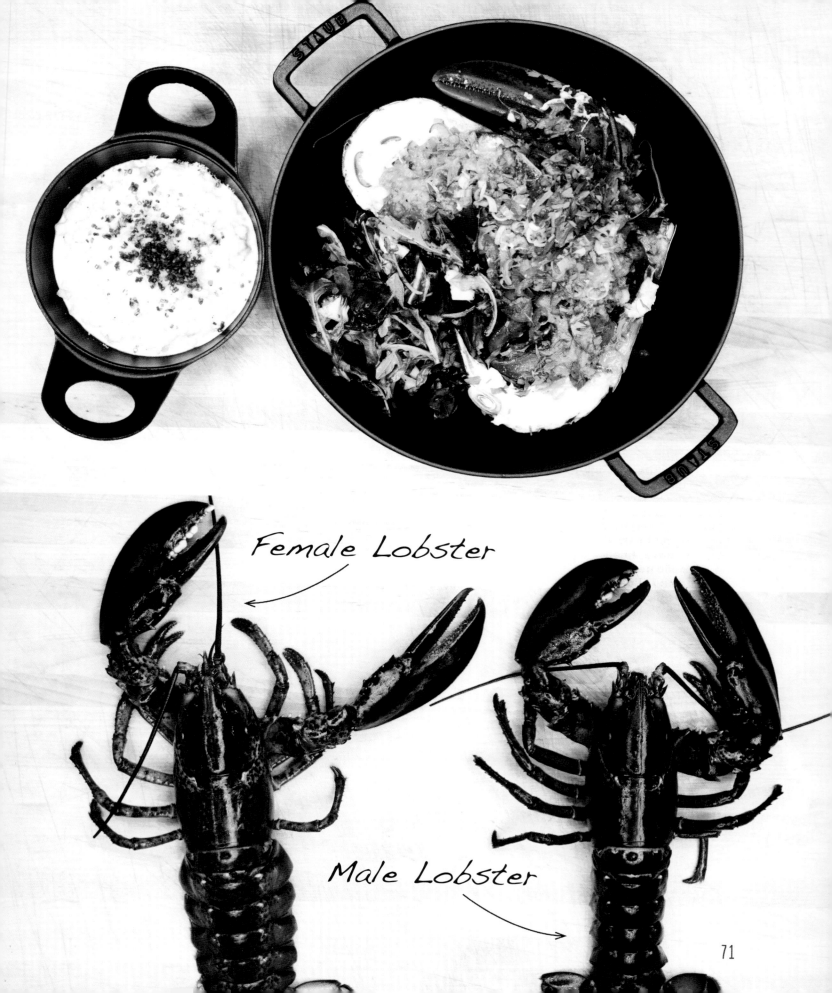

Female Lobster

Male Lobster

71

GENERAL TAO LOBSTER

Prep: 30 min -- Cook: 10 min -- Serves: 4

At least once a week after service we end up in Chinatown eating General Tao chicken. This is our nod to late nights in Montreal Chinese restaurants.

GENERAL TAO SAUCE
> 1 cup (250 mL) hoisin sauce
> ½ cup (125 mL) tamarind pulp
> zest and juice of 2 oranges
> 1 inch (2.5 cm) fresh ginger, peeled and grated
> 1 fresh bird's eye chili, finely chopped
> 1 garlic clove, finely chopped
> 1 kaffir lime leaf, crushed
> ½ tsp (2 mL) Sichuan peppercorns, ground, or to taste

LOBSTERS
> 4 small lobsters
> canola or peanut oil for deep-frying
> ½ cup (125 mL) flour
> ½ cup (125 mL) cornstarch
> salt and freshly ground pepper

For the General Tao sauce:
1. In a small saucepan, whisk together all the sauce ingredients. Bring to a boil, then simmer for 2 minutes, stirring until the sauce thickens. Set aside.

For the lobsters:
2. Plunge the lobsters into a large pot of boiling salted water and cook for 5 minutes. Dunk them in a bowl of ice water to cool slightly, then crack the shells and remove the meat. Chop lobster meat into bite-size pieces. (Reserve the shells if you want to make some lobster stock; see recipe p. 105.)

3. Meanwhile, heat the oil in a deep-fryer or large, deep pot to 350°F (180°C).

4. In a bowl combine the flour, cornstarch, salt, and pepper. Lightly dredge the lobster meat in the mixture.

5. Fry the lobster meat for 2 minutes or until crispy at the edges. Drain on paper towels.

6. Serve the lobster with sticky black rice, bok choy, snow peas, and the General Tao sauce.

NOTE
Make tamarind pulp by soaking part of a block of tamarind paste in some hot water to cover. Mash and press through a sieve.

BEEF TARTARE

Prep: 15 min -- Cook: 5 min -- Serves: 4

Ask your butcher for his best sirloin or other excellent lean cut—eye of round works well. If you work cleanly, fast, and efficiently, you will be rewarded with a delicious dish of tartare. This version is inspired by one of my favourite Montreal chefs, Marie-Fleur St-Pierre of Tapeo.

BEEF TARTARE
> 1 lb (450 g) beef sirloin, diced
> 2 shallots, thinly sliced
> ½ cup (125 mL) garlic-stuffed olives, sliced
> 1 cup (250 mL) diced Parmigiano-Reggiano
> 1 handful celery leaves
> 1 handful finely chopped chives
> 1 handful chopped parsley
> 3 tbsp (45 mL) olive oil
> green hot sauce, to taste
> salt and freshly ground pepper

FRITES WITH SMOKED SALT
> canola or peanut oil for deep-frying
> 2 Yukon Gold potatoes (unpeeled), julienned
> smoked salt
> freshly ground pepper

For the beef tartare:
1. Thoroughly combine all the tartare ingredients. Set aside.

For the frites with smoked salt:
2. Heat the oil in a deep-fryer or large, deep pot to 350°F (180°C).

3. Fry the potatoes until golden. Drain on paper towels and season with smoked salt and pepper.

4. Spoon the beef tartare onto plates and serve the smoky salted frites alongside.

JERK CRAB

Prep: 10 min -- Cook: 5 min -- Serves: 4

So spicy, so messy, so good!

- > ¼ cup (60 mL) water
- > ¼ cup (60 mL) butter
- > 1 shallot, finely chopped
- > 4 sprigs rosemary
- > 10 slices fresh ginger
- > 20 crab legs (about 6 hands or cracked sections)
- > 1 tbsp (15 mL) jerk seasoning
- > 4 limes, cut in half
- > ¼ cup (60 mL) chopped parsley leaves
- > 2 tbsp (30 mL) chopped celery leaves
- > salt and freshly ground pepper

1. Preheat the oven to 450°F (230°C).

2. In a large ovenproof skillet, bring the water and butter to a boil. Add the shallot, rosemary, and ginger. Then add the crab legs and jerk seasoning.

3. Squeeze in the juice from 2 of the limes. Add the lime halves to the pan. Stir until the crab is thoroughly coated with the spices and the cooking liquid.

4. Put the pan in the oven for 2 to 3 minutes or until the crab is warm and infused with the herbs and spices. Stir in the parsley and celery leaves and season with salt and pepper. Garnish with the remaining lime halves.

NOTE
At the restaurant we use snow crab from Havre-Saint-Pierre.

Snow crab is small and sweet. Alaskan crab legs are larger, have more meat, and are saltier. Both are very good. It's a matter of taste.

SMOKED MACKEREL WITH STEWED TOMATOES AND PAN-GRILLED GARLIC BREAD

Prep: 15 min -- Cook: 1 h -- Serves: 4

We get our smoked mackerel from a producer on Les Îles-de-la-Madeleine. It's the best you'll ever taste. You can use smoked trout or herring instead, if you like.

SMOKED MACKEREL WITH STEWED TOMATOES
> 6 onions, minced
> 1/2 cup (125 mL) + 3 tbsp (45 mL) olive oil
> 8 vine-ripened tomatoes, quartered
> 1 cup (250 mL) veal stock (see recipe p. 106)
> ¼ cup (60 mL) brown sugar
> ¼ cup (60 mL) red wine vinegar
> 2 tbsp (30 mL) duck fat
> leaves from 6 sprigs thyme, chopped
> salt and freshly ground pepper
> 1 handful chopped chives
> 1 handful chopped parsley
> 8 slices smoked mackerel

PAN-GRILLED GARLIC BREAD
> 4 cloves roasted garlic (see recipe p. 96)
> 4 thick slices country loaf
> salt and freshly ground pepper
> 2 tbsp (30 mL) olive oil

For the smoked mackerel with stewed tomatoes:
1. In a large saucepan, sauté the onions in 3 tbsp (45 mL) of the olive oil on high heat, stirring constantly until golden, about 10 minutes. Add the tomatoes, veal stock, brown sugar, red wine vinegar, duck fat, thyme, and the remaining ½ cup (125 mL) olive oil. Season with salt and pepper. Simmer for about 45 minutes, stirring once in a while, until the mixture has a compote-like texture. Add the chives and the parsley at the end. Place the slices of mackerel, flesh side down, over the stewed tomatoes. Turn off the burner. The heat from the stewed tomatoes will warm the mackerel to a melt-in-your-mouth consistency.

For the pan-grilled garlic bread:
2. While the tomatoes are simmering, spread the roasted garlic on each slice of bread. Season with salt and pepper. In a large skillet, heat the olive oil over medium-high heat. Add the bread and toast it until golden.

3. Place a piece of toast on each plate and ladle the stewed tomatoes over the toast. Top each serving with 2 slices of smoked mackerel.

NOTE
At the restaurant we use smoked mackerel from the Fumoir d'Antan of Îles-de-la-Madeleine. You can find their products at just about any good fishmonger, if you happen to live in La Belle Province. Otherwise, choose any good smoked mackerel from your local fishmonger.

I add duck fat to the stewed tomatoes for a more gourmand flavour (meaty taste). It truly does add another dimension to this dish. Otherwise, it's just a tomato, a slice of bread, and a piece of fish . . .

DUCK BREAST AND FOIE GRAS IN RED WINE SAUCE

Prep: 10 min -- Cook: 25 min -- Serves: 4

FINGERLING POTATOES
> 1 lb (450 g) fingerling potatoes, cut in half lengthwise
> 2 tbsp (30 mL) olive oil
> ½ lb (225 g) chanterelle mushrooms, torn gently
> kernels from 2 cobs of corn (in season)
> 2 cups (500 mL) red wine sauce (see recipe p. 126)
> ¼ cup (60 mL) butter, diced
> salt and freshly ground pepper
> 2 tbsp (30 mL) thinly sliced chives
> 2 tbsp (30 mL) chopped parsley

DUCK BREASTS
> 2 duck breasts
> salt and freshly ground pepper

DUCK FOIE GRAS
> 4 slices duck foie gras
> salt and freshly ground pepper
--
> 4 slices Riopelle or other triple-crème cheese
> Maldon sea salt

For the fingerling potatoes:
1. Boil the potatoes in salted water until just tender, about 20 minutes. Drain.

2. In a large skillet, heat the olive oil on medium and brown the potatoes. Add the mushrooms and sauté the mixture until the mushrooms are tender and beginning to brown. Add the corn and red wine sauce and continue cooking for 5 minutes, until corn is tender. Swirl in in the butter, one piece at a time. Season with salt and pepper. Add the chives and parsley. Set aside and keep warm.

For the duck breasts:
3. Preheat the oven to 450°F (230°C).

4. Score the duck skin without cutting through to the meat. Turn the breast meat side up and cut away any fat hanging over the sides around the meat. Season both sides with salt and pepper. (If you prefer, you can remove the tender.*) Heat an ovenproof skillet on high, then cook the breasts, skin side down, until golden and crispy. Put the pan in the oven and continue cooking for 8 minutes (for rare). Remove from the oven and cover with foil to keep warm.

For the duck foie gras:
5. Season the foie gras with salt and pepper. In a very hot cast-iron pan, sear the foie gras for 1 minute on each side.

6. Slice the duck breasts. Spoon the vegetables and the sauce onto plates. Top with a slice of Riopelle, slices of duck breast, and a slice of foie gras. Season the foie gras with Maldon sea salt.

NOTE
Don't hesitate to play around with this recipe. You can personalize it depending on seasonal produce.

Depending on the time of year, I use oven-baked Yukon Gold potatoes, which I top with a slice of Riopelle cheese.

I sometimes use peeled, sliced salsify, which I caramelize in the oven in a mixture of reduced veal stock and whipped butter.

*Removing the duck tender is simply a matter of aesthetics. The meat is very moist and succulent, perfect for tartare or carpaccio.

LOBSTER POUTINE

Prep: 15 min -- Cook: 30 min -- Serves: 4

When we opened the restaurant we had a weekly lobster dish, such as lobster pot pie, lobster risotto, or General Tao lobster. But back in the kitchen the boys always used to make themselves fries with lobster gravy and cheese curds. Voilà—a classic was born.

> **4 lobsters, each 1 to 1½ lb (500 to 675 g)**
> **4 cups (1 L) lobster stock (see recipe p. 105)**
> **2 tbsp (30 mL) butter**
> **salt and freshly ground pepper**
> **canola or peanut oil for deep-frying**
> **6 Yukon Gold potatoes (unpeeled), julienned**
> **1 lb (450 g) cheese curds**
> **finely chopped chives, for garnish**

1. In a large pot of boiling salted water, cook the lobsters for 2 minutes. Cool in ice water. Remove meat from the shell and set the lobster meat aside. (If you do this ahead of time, chill the lobster meat and use the shells for making the lobster stock.)

2. For the gravy, reduce the lobster stock by half until it is thick enough to coat a spoon. Whisk in the butter a spoonful at a time. Season with salt and pepper. Add the lobster meat and gently reheat it while you make the frites.

3. For the frites, heat the oil in a deep-fryer or large, deep pot to 300°F (150°C).

4. Dunk the potatoes in the hot oil for 2 to 3 minutes to blanch them. Drain and let sit for a few minutes. Heat the same oil to 350°F (180°C). Cook the frites 2 to 3 minutes more, until golden and crispy. Drain on paper towels and season with salt and pepper.

5. Top the frites with the cheese curds and lobster gravy. Garnish with chives.

ROCK SHRIMP RISOTTO AND LOBSTER BROTH

Prep: 30 min -- Cook: 30 min -- Serves: 4

We made a version of this dish with lobster on *Iron Chef*; it helped us win against the (almost) unbeatable Bobby Flay.

LOBSTER BROTH
> 4 cups (1 L) lobster stock (see recipe p. 105)
> 2 tbsp (30 mL) butter, diced
> salt and freshly ground pepper

RISOTTO
> 1 onion, finely chopped
> 1 tbsp (15 mL) olive oil
> 2 cups (500 mL) arborio rice
> 4 cups (1 L) water
> 1 lb (450 g) rock shrimp, peeled and deveined
> ¼ cup (60 mL) butter, diced
> 1 cup (250 mL) grated Parmigiano-Reggiano
> salt and freshly ground pepper

SAUTÉED MUSHROOMS
> 2 tbsp (30 mL) olive oil
> 1 lb (450 g) assorted mushrooms (shiitake, oyster, chanterelle, bunashimeji, etc.), cleaned gently and torn or sliced if necessary
> 1 shallot, chopped
> 1 garlic clove, chopped
> salt and freshly ground pepper

For the lobster broth:
1. In a pot bring the lobster stock to a boil, then simmer on medium heat for 30 minutes until reduced by half. Whisk in the butter, a few cubes at a time. Season with salt and pepper.

For the risotto:
2. In a large saucepan, sauté the onions in the oil until they are transparent, about 5 minutes. Add the rice and stir it until it is coated with the oil. Add 1 cup (250 mL) of the water, stirring constantly until all the liquid is absorbed. Continue adding water 1 cup (250 mL) at a time, stirring constantly and ensuring that the rice absorbs the liquid before adding more. Continue to do this until the rice is tender and creamy but still al dente, about 20 minutes.

3. About 5 minutes before the rice is done, add the rock shrimp.

4. On low heat, add the butter and Parmesan. Season with salt and pepper. Set aside and keep warm.

For the sautéed mushrooms:
5. Heat the olive oil in a large skillet over high heat. Sauté the mushrooms with the shallot and the garlic until the mushrooms are golden. Season with salt and pepper. Set aside.

6. Spoon the risotto onto plates, spoon the mushrooms over the risotto, and ladle on the lobster broth.

NOTE
At the restaurant we parcook our risotto so that it's a little more than halfway done. We finish cooking and flavouring it at the last minute.

Make crab arancini with any leftover risotto (see recipe p. 58).

ROAST SUCKLING PIG

Prep: 15 min -- Cook: 2 h -- Serves: 8 to 10

Suckling pig is great for a special occasion—yes, you can do it! The pig cooks low and slow in your oven so you can get on with hosting a big party!

> 1 suckling pig, about 10 lb (4.5 kg)
> salt and freshly ground pepper
> 3 tbsp (45 mL) canola oil
> ½ lb (225 g) bacon, diced
> 8 carrots, cut in half lengthwise
> 8 parsley roots, cut in half lengthwise
> 6 shallots, cut in half lengthwise
> 4 garlic cloves (unpeeled), cut in half
> 2 cups (500 mL) shelled fresh romano beans
> a few sprigs rosemary

1. Preheat the oven to 350°F (180°C).

2. Have your butcher score the skin and fat of the suckling pig. Season the suckling pig with salt and pepper. In a large roasting pan, heat the oil and brown the meat on all sides. Set aside on a plate.

3. In the same pan, briefly sauté the bacon, carrots, parsley roots, shallots, and garlic until aromatic. Add the romano beans and rosemary. Put the suckling pig back in the pan and roast for 2 hours.

4. Carve the meat and serve with the roasted vegetables and with mashed roasted garlic potatoes (see recipe p. 169).

NOTE
You can serve this roast with red wine sauce (see recipe p. 126). Or you can simply deglaze the pan with red wine and veal stock (see recipe p. 106), then whisk in a little butter.

▶

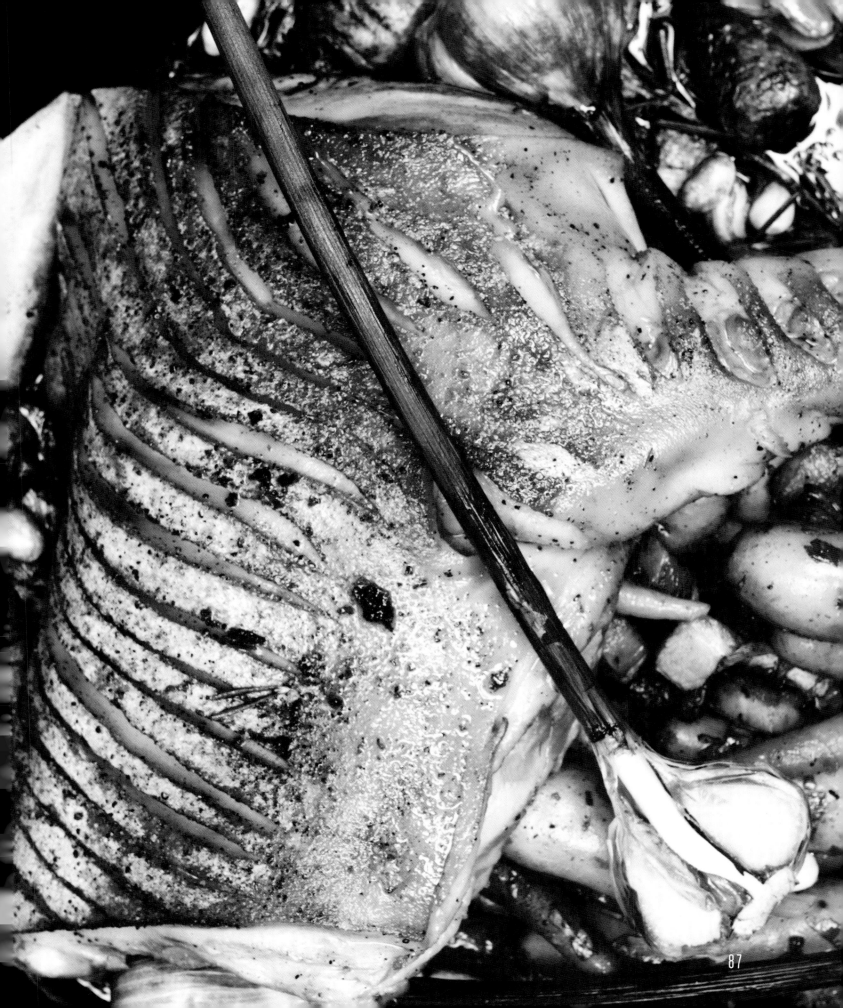

WRECKFISH
AND LAUGHING BIRD SHRIMP SALAD

Prep: 45 min -- Cook: 15 min -- Serves: 4

Wreckfish is from North Carolina, where it swims among the old shipwrecks (hence its name). It's closely related to grouper, definitely one of my favourite fish.

WRECKFISH
> 4 skin-on wreckfish fillets, each ⅓ lb (150 g)
> salt and freshly ground pepper
> 2 tbsp (30 mL) canola oil

LAUGHING BIRD SHRIMP SALAD
> ½ lb (225 g) Laughing Bird shrimp
> salt and freshly ground pepper
> 1 cup (250 mL) cucumber salad (see recipe p. 118)
> 1 cup (250 mL) fennel salad (see recipe p. 118)
> 1 cup (250 mL) julienned radishes
> 4 handfuls arugula
> 3 tbsp (45 mL) trout caviar (roe)
> 1 tbsp (15 mL) chopped dill
> 1 tbsp (15 mL) chopped chives
> 1 tbsp (15 mL) chopped parsley

GARNISH
> ¼ cup (60 mL) black garlic salsa (see recipe p. 124)

For the wreckfish:
1. Preheat the oven to 350°F (180°C).

2. Season the fillets with salt and pepper. In a cast-iron skillet, cook the fish, skin side down, in very hot oil for 1 minute, pressing lightly with a spatula so the fillets cook evenly. Turn the fish over, transfer the pan to the oven, and continue cooking for 5 minutes or more, to taste. Transfer to a plate, cover with foil, and set aside.

For the shrimp salad:
3. Add a little oil to the skillet if needed. Over high heat, sauté the shrimp just until cooked. Season with salt and pepper. Transfer to a bowl and add the cucumber salad, fennel salad, radishes, arugula, trout caviar, dill, chives, and parsley. Toss well.

4. Serve the fish with a spoonful of black garlic salsa and the shrimp salad.

NOTE
Wreckfish is a firm-fleshed white fish weighing between 15 and 20 lb (6.75 to 9 kg). This makes it easy to fillet into large pieces. Wreckfish meat is very tender and flaky.

You can use any other white fish, providing it's firm-fleshed.

BEEF SHORT RIBS WITH CAMBOZOLA

Prep: 15 min -- Cook: 4 h 30 -- Serves: 4

Short ribs were the focus of the very first episode of *Chuck's Day Off*. I got so much mail about that recipe; it's definitely one of the most popular dishes I've ever done. Braising short ribs is so easy, and it makes you look like a rock star. This is one of many variations.

> 4 beef short ribs
> salt and freshly ground pepper
> 2 carrots, chopped
> 4 celery ribs, chopped
> 1 onion, chopped
> 1 red beet, peeled and sliced
> 1 handful thyme sprigs
> 1 handful rosemary sprigs
> ½ cup (125 mL) brown sugar
> 8 cups (2 L) red wine
> ¼ cup (60 mL) butter, diced
> 4 slices Cambozola cheese

NOTE
You can use Riopelle or Camembert instead of Cambozola.

1. Preheat the oven to 350°F (180°C).

2. Season the short ribs with salt and pepper. In a roasting pan on high heat, brown the short ribs on all sides. Add the vegetables; cook for a few minutes to caramelize. Add the herbs, brown sugar, and red wine.

3. Cover, transfer to the oven, and braise for 4 hours or until a fork is all you need to take the meat off the bone.

4. Set the meat aside and keep warm. Press the vegetables through a fine sieve to extract all the flavours. Pour this liquid into a saucepan. Remove the surface fat with a ladle. Bring the liquid to a boil and reduce by half or until the sauce is thick enough to coat a spoon. Whisk in the butter, a few pieces at a time.

5. Top some mashed potatoes with a short rib, add a slice of Cambozola, and spoon over some sauce.

ARDE-MANGER

GARDE-MANGER

--
My very first job in a restaurant was in the larder.
I was a "garde-manger," or "keeper of the food."

The larder is not only where ingredients of all kinds
are kept. It is also the name given to the person
who is responsible for its contents. Working in the
larder is usually a beginner's job, one that trains you
in the preparation of fish, seafood, meats, sauces,
vinaigrettes, vegetables, and desserts. The garde-
manger also sees to the proper stocking of the larder.
Whatever the restaurant might need, he or she finds it.

To this day, the job of garde-manger in
the larder remains my favourite.

ROASTED GARLIC

Prep: 5 min -- Cook: 30 min -- Makes: 2 heads

At the restaurant we go through 150 to 200 heads of garlic each week. Sweet and smoky, roasted garlic is the bomb.

> **2 heads garlic**
> **1 tbsp (15 mL) olive oil**
> **salt and freshly ground pepper**

1. Preheat the oven to 400°F (200°C).

2. Cut enough off the top of the heads of garlic to expose the cloves inside. Drizzle with the olive oil and season with salt and pepper. Wrap the garlic heads in foil and roast them for about 30 minutes or until they are soft. Let cool.

NOTE

The garlic will keep, in an airtight container in the fridge, for about a week.

Roasted garlic is a basic ingredient in quite a number of dishes. You could serve it with preserved pork belly, for example (see recipe p. 62).

CARROT BUTTER

Prep: 10 min -- Cook: 30 min -- Serves: 4

> **8 to 10 large carrots**
> **1 tsp (5 mL) cornstarch**
> **½ lb (225 g) butter, diced**
> **salt and freshly ground pepper**

1. Put the carrots in a juicer to extract 4 cups (1 L) carrot juice.

2. Transfer the carrot juice to a saucepan, whisk in the cornstarch, and boil until reduced to 1 cup (250 mL).

3. Reduce heat and whisk in the diced butter a few pieces at a time. Remove from heat and season with salt and pepper.

NOTE

You can use store-bought carrot juice if you don't have a juicer.

Carrot butter is delicious on scallops, vegetarian risotto, sautéed mushrooms, lobster, or white fish. It is one of our signature sauces, much appreciated by vegetarians.

LOBSTER BUTTER

Prep: 5 min -- Cook: 5 min -- Makes: 1 lb [450 g]

The restaurant's secret weapon: we use this in most of our seafood recipes to add depth and complex flavours.

> **1 lb (450 g) butter**
> **roe from 1 female lobster***

In a saucepan, melt the butter. Whisk in the roe.

NOTE

The butter keeps, in an airtight container in the fridge, for up to 3 months, or you can freeze it for up to 6 months.

I don't strain lobster butter—it really isn't necessary. The roe remains on the bottom and the butter on top.

*Whenever you cook a female lobster, use the roe to make this butter.

This butter is red. You can use it in a grilled cheese sandwich with bacon and seafood. You can sauté perogies in it, use it on pasta, brush it on grilled scallops, or stir it into a risotto. You can sauté vegetables like rapini with lobster butter, use it on corn or on a steak (for surf & turf) . . . go wild!

SEASONED SOUR CREAM

Prep: 5 min -- Makes: 1 1/4 cups [300 mL]

> **1 cup (250 mL) sour cream**
> **zest and juice of 3 lemons**
> **salt and freshly ground pepper**

Mix all the ingredients in a bowl.

NOTE

Store in an airtight container in the refrigerator for up to 3 days.

We use a lot of seasoned sour cream—it is a basic ingredient at the restaurant. It's delicious with seafood.

CROUTONS

Prep: 5 min -- Cook: about 10 min -- Makes: 2 to 3 cups (500 to 750 mL)

STEAK SPICE CROUTONS

> 2 tbsp (30 mL) olive oil
> 2 tbsp (30 mL) butter, melted
> 1 tbsp (15 mL) steak spices
  (see recipe p. 101 or use
  store-bought)
> 4 thick slices country loaf,
  coarsely cubed

1. Preheat the oven to 400°F (200°C).

2. Combine the oil, butter, and steak spices in a large bowl. Add the bread and toss to coat well. Spread on a baking sheet and bake until croutons are golden and crisp, about 10 minutes.

NOTE
You can keep steak spice croutons, in an airtight container, for up to a week. At the restaurant we use them in a number of recipes.

BLUE CHEESE CROUTONS

> 4 thick slices country loaf
> 4 thin slices Cambozola cheese

1. Preheat the oven to 400°F (200°C).

2. Top each slice of bread with a slice of Cambozola. Put on a baking sheet and bake until the cheese melts. Cut into large cubes.

NOTE
Serve on fennel salad (see recipe p. 118) with tomatoes poached in olive oil (see recipe p. 60).

BANANA NUT BREAD CROUTONS

> leftover banana nut bread,
  cubed
> butter (about 1 tbsp/15 mL for
  every 2 slices of banana bread)

In a skillet, sauté the banana bread in the butter until crispy and golden.

NOTE
Serve with fruit salad topped with lemon or coconut yogurt.

STEAK SPICES

Prep: 5 min -- Makes: about 1/2 cup (125 mL)

> **2 tbsp (30 mL) coarse salt**
> **2 tbsp (30 mL) coriander seeds**
> **2 tbsp (30 mL) black peppercorns**
> **2 tbsp (30 mL) pink peppercorns**
> **1 tbsp (15 mL) dried garlic**
> **1 tbsp (15 mL) dried onion flakes**
> **1 tsp (5 mL) hot pepper flakes**
> **1 tsp (5 mL) mustard seeds**

Crush all the ingredients with a mortar and pestle. Store in an airtight container and use within a couple of weeks for best flavour.

CHICKEN STOCK

Prep: 30 min -- Cook: 6 h -- Makes: 4 cups (1 L)

> 3 tbsp (45 mL) canola oil
> 1 chicken carcass
> 6 carrots, coarsely chopped
> 4 celery ribs, coarsely chopped
> 2 onions (unpeeled), cut in half
> 2 leeks (white and pale green parts only), coarsely chopped
> 1 head garlic, cut in half crosswise
> 4 sprigs thyme
> 4 sprigs rosemary
> 1 bunch flat-leaf parsley
> 1 handful dill
> 1 tbsp (15 mL) black peppercorns
> 16 cups (4 L) water
> salt and freshly ground pepper

In a stock pot, heat the oil over medium-high. Add the chicken carcass and brown it on all sides, about 5 minutes. Add the vegetables, herbs, and peppercorns. Cook for 10 minutes, until the vegetables are soft. Add the water and simmer very gently, uncovered, for 6 hours, skimming off any scum that rises to the surface. Strain the stock and skim off any fat. If necessary, simmer until reduced to 4 cups (1 L). Season with salt and pepper.

NOTE
You can keep chicken stock in the fridge for up to a week or up to 3 months in the freezer.

LOBSTER STOCK

Prep: 15 min -- Cook: 2 h 30 -- Makes: 4 cups (1 L)

> 2 lobsters, each 1½ lb (675 g)
> 3 tbsp (45 mL) olive oil
> 1 carrot, chopped
> 1 onion, chopped
> 1 celery rib, chopped
> 1 head garlic, cut in half crosswise
> 4 sprigs rosemary
> 4 sprigs thyme
> 2 tbsp (30 mL) ketchup
> 1 tbsp (15 mL) black peppercorns
> 8 cups (2 L) water
> sea salt

1. In a large pot of boiling salted water, cook the lobsters for 6 to 7 minutes. Put them in a bowl of ice water to stop them from cooking further. When they're cool enough to handle, shell them and remove the meat. Set aside the shells. (Use the meat immediately in one of the lobster recipes or refrigerate it for later use.)

2. In the same pot, heat the oil over medium heat. Add the carrot, onion, celery, and garlic; sweat, stirring constantly, for 5 minutes. Add the lobster shells, rosemary, thyme, ketchup, and peppercorns; continue cooking for 10 minutes, stirring constantly. Add the water and simmer, uncovered, for 2 hours.

3. Strain the stock, transfer it to a saucepan, and simmer until reduced to 4 cups (1 L). Season with salt.

NOTE

You can keep lobster broth in the fridge for up to a week or up to 3 months in the freezer.

Use this stock to make the sauce for lobster poutine (see recipe p. 82).

VEAL STOCK

Prep: 30 min -- Cook: 11 h -- Makes: 4 cups (1 L)

- > **8 veal bones**
- > **salt and freshly ground pepper**
- > **3 tbsp (45 mL) canola oil**
- > **1 tbsp (15 mL) tomato paste**
- > **1 head garlic, cut in half crosswise**
- > **6 carrots, coarsely chopped**
- > **2 onions (unpeeled), cut in half**
- > **4 celery ribs, coarsely chopped**
- > **2 leeks (white and pale green parts only), coarsely chopped**
- > **4 sprigs thyme**
- > **4 sprigs rosemary**
- > **1 bunch flat-leaf parsley**
- > **1 tbsp (15 mL) black peppercorns**
- > **16 cups + 1 cup (4.25 L) water**

1. Preheat the oven to 450°F (230°C).

2. Put the veal bones in a large roasting pan. Season with salt and pepper and drizzle with oil. Roast for 1 hour, turning them over halfway through. Spoon the tomato paste onto the bones. Scatter the garlic, carrots, onions, celery, and leeks around the bones. Roast for another hour or until all the vegetables are caramelized, stirring halfway through.

3. Transfer the bones and roasted vegetables to a stock pot. Add the thyme, rosemary, parsley, peppercorns, and 16 cups (4 L) of water. Remove the fat from the roasting pan and put the pan over medium heat. Add the remaining 1 cup (250 mL) of water and bring to a boil, scraping the bottom of the pan with a wooden spoon to dissolve the brown bits. Add this liquid to the stock pot. Simmer over low heat for 8 hours, skimming the broth frequently during the first hour.

4. Strain the stock into a large pot. Skim the fat from the surface. Simmer until the stock is reduced to 4 cups (1 L), about 1 hour. Season to taste.

NOTE

You can keep veal stock for up to a week in the fridge or up to 3 months in the freezer.

PEROGIES

Prep: 30 min -- Cook: 15 min -- Makes: 72

> 4 Yukon Gold potatoes,
  boiled and mashed
> 1 cup (250 mL) 35%
  cream, heated
> 6 green onions, finely chopped
> ¼ cup (60 mL) grated
  Parmigiano-Reggiano
> salt and freshly ground pepper
> 1 pkg (72 sheets) round
  wonton wrappers

1. In a bowl, combine the potatoes,
   cream, green onions, Parmesan,
   and salt and pepper. Mix
   well. Set aside in the fridge
   for 30 minutes to solidify.

2. With a pastry brush, wet the edges
   of the wonton wrappers with water.
   Place 1 tsp (5 mL) of the potato
   mixture on a wrapper, slightly
   off-centre, fold over the wrapper,
   pushing out excess air, and pinch
   the edges to seal. Place on a baking
   sheet lined with parchment paper.

3. In a pot of boiling salted water, cook
   the perogies in batches for 3 to 4
   minutes or until tender. Drain.

NOTE
You can freeze uncooked perogies
for up to 3 months. Don't thaw
them before cooking.

For an extra touch, add butter
to the boiling water.

Perogies can also be deep-fried for
a few minutes until they are crispy
and golden. Drain on paper towels
and season with salt and pepper.

WAFFLES

Prep: 15 min -- Cook: 15 min -- Serves: 4

- **2 cups (500 mL) unbleached flour**
- **1 tbsp (15 mL) baking powder**
- **pinch salt**
- **3 eggs, separated**
- **2 cups (500 mL) sour cream**
- **½ cup (125 mL) milk**
- **¼ cup (60 mL) butter, melted**

1. Combine the flour, baking powder, and salt in a bowl. In another bowl, whip the egg whites into soft mounds.

2. In a third bowl, stir together the sour cream, milk, butter, and egg yolks. Add to the dry ingredients, stirring just until combined. Gently fold in the egg whites.

3. Preheat a waffle iron. Use ½ cup (125 mL) of the batter for each waffle (manufacturers' instructions may vary). Cook for 5 minutes or until the waffles are golden brown. Set aside and keep warm. Repeat with the remaining batter.

NOTE

Waffles can be either sweet or savoury. We use them in our fried hot chicken on waffles (see recipe p. 68).

MAYONNAISES

Prep: 5 min -- Makes: about 1 1/2 cups (375 mL)

BASIC MAYONNAISE
> 1 egg
> 1½ tsp (7 mL) Dijon mustard
> juice of ½ lemon (or 1½ tsp/ 7 mL red wine vinegar or red wine vinegar mignonnette —see recipe p. 112)
> 1 cup (250 mL) canola oil
> salt and freshly ground pepper

In a blender or food processor, combine the egg, mustard, and lemon juice. With the motor running, drizzle in the oil until the mayonnaise has set. Season with salt and pepper.

NOTE
You can keep mayonnaise in the fridge for up to 5 days.

Jerk Mayonnaise
Add 1 tbsp (15 mL) jerk seasoning to 1 cup (250 mL) basic mayonnaise.

Spicy Mayonnaise
Add 1 tbsp (15 mL) Sriracha sauce to 1 cup (250 mL) basic mayonnaise.

Smoked Paprika Mayonnaise
Add 1 tsp (5 mL) smoked paprika to 1 cup (250 mL) basic mayonnaise.

Chipotle Mayonnaise
Finely chop 1 chipotle pepper in adobo sauce and mix with 1 cup (250 mL) basic mayonnaise.

Horseradish and Roasted Garlic Mayonnaise
Add 1 tbsp (15 mL) grated fresh horseradish (or prepared, if necessary), 2 cloves roasted garlic (see recipe p. 96), and the zest of 1 lemon to 1 cup (250 mL) basic mayonnaise.

Smoked Tomato Mayonnaise
Add 1 tsp (5 mL) smoked tomato vinaigrette (see recipe p. 135) to 1 cup (250 mL) basic mayonnaise.

Roasted Tomato Mayonnaise
Finely chop 2 preserved tomato halves (see recipe p. 134) and add to 1 cup (250 mL) basic mayonnaise.

Cocktail Sauce Mayonnaise
Add 1 tbsp (15 mL) cocktail sauce (see recipe p. 128) to 1 cup (250 mL) basic mayonnaise.

Jalapeño Mayonnaise
Finely chop 4 marinated jalapeño pepper slices (see recipe p. 114) and mix with 1 cup (250 mL) basic mayonnaise.

Dill Mayonnaise
Add 1 tbsp (15 mL) finely chopped dill to 1 cup (250 mL) basic mayonnaise.

WHITE BALSAMIC MIGNONNETTE

Prep: 5 min -- Makes: 1 cup (250 mL)

> **1 cup (250 mL) white balsamic vinegar**
> **1 shallot, finely chopped**

Mix the ingredients in a jar.

RED WINE VINEGAR MIGNONNETTE

Prep: 5 min -- Makes: 1 cup (250 mL)

> **1 cup (250 mL) red wine vinegar**
> **1 tsp (5 mL) crushed black peppercorns**
> **1 shallot, finely chopped**

Mix the ingredients in a jar.

NOTE

These mignonnettes keep well in the fridge. Use within 2 weeks.

At the restaurant we serve mignonnette with fresh oysters and a couple of lemon wedges. I also use it to flavour mayonnaise.

PRALINE PECANS

Prep: 5 min -- Cook: 5 min -- Makes: 2 cups (500 mL)

> 1 cup (250 mL) sugar
> 2 tbsp (30 mL) water
> 2 cups (500 mL) pecans
> Maldon sea salt

1. Line a baking sheet with parchment paper.

2. In a small saucepan, bring the sugar and water to a boil, stirring gently with a fork until the sugar dissolves. Cook until the caramel is golden, gently swirling the pan to help it colour evenly.

3. Remove from heat, add the pecans, and quickly stir with a wooden spoon to coat the nuts. Quickly spread these on the baking sheet. Season with the salt. Let cool. Break into pieces.

NOTE

These pecans are a wonderful garnish for desserts and delicious in salads. They also make an excellent snack.

The pecans will keep, in an airtight container at room temperature, for several weeks.

MARINATED JALAPEÑO PEPPERS

Prep: 10 min -- Cook: 10 min

> ½ lb (225 g) jalapeño peppers, sliced
> 2 cups (500 mL) cider vinegar
> 1 cup (250 mL) sugar

1. In a pot of boiling water, blanch the jalapeños for 30 seconds. Drain the peppers. Pour fresh water into the pot and repeat this step twice to reduce the intensity of the peppers. (If you like them very spicy, blanch them only once.)

2. In the same pot bring the vinegar and sugar to a boil, stirring until the sugar has dissolved. Add the jalapeños and simmer for 1 minute. Pour into jars.

NOTE

The peppers keep for up to 2 weeks refrigerated.

At the restaurant, we use these peppers in our shrimp roll (see recipe p. 192) and add them to our spicy lobster (see p. 70) as well as our jerk crab (see p. 76).

These jalapeño slices are great in a martini, in spaghetti sauce, on a hamburger, with roast chicken—you name it.

FENNEL SALAD

Prep: 5 min -- Serves: 4

> 1 fennel bulb, thinly sliced with a mandoline
> 2 tbsp (30 mL) olive oil
> juice of 2 lemons
> salt and freshly ground pepper

Toss together all the ingredients.

NOTE

This salad is great with a number of our recipes, such as wreckfish and Laughing Bird shrimp salad (see recipe p. 88) and sardines and roasted tomatoes on toast (see recipe p. 50).

CUCUMBER SALAD

Prep: 5 min -- Serves: 4

> 2 English cucumbers, peeled and thinly sliced
> 2 big handfuls chopped dill
> ¼ cup (60 mL) white vinegar
> 2 tbsp (30 mL) sugar
> 1 garlic clove, minced
> 1 tsp (5 mL) salt
> freshly ground pepper

Toss together all the ingredients.

NOTE

This salad is wonderful on its own. You can also mix it with other salads or use it as a garnish on fish or any kind of fowl.

This is Chris's mom's recipe. He works with us at the restaurant.

CELERIAC RÉMOULADE

Prep: 5 min -- Serves: 4

> **1 large celeriac, peeled**
> **¼ cup (60 mL) basic mayonnaise (see recipe p. 111)**
> **2 tbsp (30 mL) Dijon mustard**
> **salt and freshly ground pepper**

With a mandoline or food processor, finely julienne the celeriac. (You should have about 3 cups/750 mL.) Mix well with the remaining ingredients.

NOTE

At Garde-Manger, we serve this rémoulade with veal cheeks in beer (see recipe p. 40).

TOMATO, AVOCADO, AND FRIED CHEDDAR SALAD

Prep: 10 min -- Cook: 5 min -- Serves: 4

One of my favourite things about cooking is creating contrast in texture, and keeping things playful. This is a basic tomato salad, but the crispy, molten Cheddar cubes take it to the next level—and they're really fun to eat.

SALAD
- > 4 large vine-ripened tomatoes, diced
- > 2 avocados, diced
- > 1 English cucumber, seeded and diced
- > 1 shallot, thinly sliced
- > 1 handful chopped basil
- > 1 handful chopped chives
- > 1 handful chopped dill
- > 3 tbsp (45 mL) olive oil
- > 2 tbsp (30 mL) white balsamic vinegar
- > salt and freshly ground pepper
- > steak spice croutons (see recipe p. 100)

FRIED CHEDDAR
- > canola oil for deep-frying
- > 1 cup (250 mL) flour
- > salt and freshly ground pepper
- > 4 eggs
- > 1 lb (450 g) aged Cheddar cheese, cut in bite-size pieces

For the salad:

1. Toss together the tomatoes, avocados, cucumber, shallot, and herbs. Add the olive oil and vinegar; toss again. Season with salt and pepper.

For the fried Cheddar:

2. Heat the oil in a deep-fryer or large, deep pot to 350°F (180°C).

3. Put the flour in a bowl and season with salt and pepper. In another bowl whisk the eggs.

4. Coat the pieces of Cheddar with the flour, tapping off any excess. Coat with the eggs, then once again with the flour. Working in batches, fry the cheese for 2 minutes or until golden. Drain on paper towels and season with salt and pepper.

5. Serve the salad topped with the croutons and the fried Cheddar.

NOTE
We use two-year-old Cheddar from Île-aux-Grues, but any good aged Cheddar will do.

During tomato season, we have a variety to choose from: cherry, yellow, red, etc.

BLACK GARLIC SALSA

Prep: 10 min -- Serves: 4

Black garlic is a Korean ingredient; it has a fermented, sweet, acidic flavour with a pungent smokiness. Serve this as you would any salsa, and wow your guests.

> cloves from 2 heads black garlic, peeled
> 1 onion, coarsely chopped
> 1 cucumber, seeded and diced
> 3 vine-ripened tomatoes, quartered and seeded
> 2 jalapeño peppers, seeded and finely chopped
> zest and juice of 1 lime
> 3 tbsp (45 mL) olive oil
> salt and freshly ground pepper

Put all the ingredients in a food processor and pulse until the mixture is combined but still has a coarse texture.

RED WINE SAUCE

Prep: 15 min -- Cook: 1 h 30 -- Serves: 4

> **4 cups (1 L) veal stock
>   (see recipe p. 106)**
> **1 shallot, chopped**
> **1 large beet, washed and cubed**
> **2 tbsp (30 mL) olive oil**
> **1 tbsp (15 mL) mustard seeds**
> **3 tbsp (45 mL) honey**
> **¼ cup (60 mL) orange juice**
> **½ cup (125 mL) sherry vinegar
>   or Banyuls vinegar**
> **4 cups (1 L) red wine**
> **¼ cup (60 mL) butter, diced**
> **salt and freshly ground pepper**

1. In a large saucepan, simmer the veal stock until it is reduced to 1 cup (250 mL).

2. Meanwhile, in a large pot on high heat, briefly sauté the shallot and the beet in the olive oil. Add the mustard seeds, honey, orange juice, and vinegar. Reduce by half. Add the red wine, lower the heat to medium, and simmer until the liquid is reduced to 1 cup (250 mL), about 1 hour. Strain through a fine sieve, pressing on the vegetables to extract the maximum amount of flavour and juice.

3. Over the next half hour, add red wine reduction to the veal stock reduction, 1 ladle at a time, letting it simmer for a while after each addition, until you get the texture and flavour you want. Whisk in the butter, a few pieces at a time. Season with salt and pepper.

NOTE

Any leftover simmered sauce is an ideal base for a new sauce. Instead of using this recipe, simply strain your simmered sauce through a sieve and whisk in some butter.

COCKTAIL SAUCE

Prep: 5 min -- Serves: 4

> **1 cup (250 mL) ketchup**
> **¼ cup (60 mL) Worcestershire sauce**
> **2 tbsp (30 mL) grated fresh horseradish**
> **1 tbsp (15 mL) prepared horseradish**
> **1 tbsp (15 mL) cognac**
> **1 tsp (5 mL) Tabasco sauce**
> **1 celery rib, finely chopped**
> **juice of 1 lemon**
> **salt and freshly ground pepper**

Mix together all the ingredients. Chill until needed.

NOTE

At the restaurant we finely chop the celery in a food processor, then squeeze the liquid from it before mixing it with the remaining ingredients.

Serve this cocktail sauce with oysters, like we do. Or treat it as a high-end ketchup with fries. Our restaurant crew loves it with their omelettes. And it's great with bib steak and other meats.

BARBECUE SAUCE

Prep: 15 min -- Cook: 1 h 30 -- Makes: 4 cups (1 L)

> 3 onions, thinly sliced
> 1 tbsp (15 mL) canola oil
> 2 cups (500 mL) ketchup
> 1 cup (250 mL) espresso or black coffee
> 1 can (165 mL) Coca-Cola
> 1 chipotle pepper in adobo sauce, finely chopped
> 1 tsp (5 mL) Worcestershire sauce
> salt and freshly ground pepper

In a large skillet over low heat, cook the onions in the oil until golden, about 45 minutes. Add the remaining ingredients. Simmer for 45 minutes, stirring once in a while. Let cool.

NOTE
Barbecue sauce will keep, refrigerated, for up to a week.

The caramelized onions are what make this sauce. Cooking them slowly on low heat brings out their natural sweetness, so their taste differs from those cooked on higher heat and with sugar. You can spread them on all kinds of things, including roast chicken.

CARAMELIZED ONION SPREAD

Prep: 10 min -- Cook: 45 min -- Makes: 3 cups (750 mL)

> ¼ cup (60 mL) olive oil
> 8 onions, thinly sliced
> 2 cups (500 mL) cream cheese, softened
> 1 tsp (5 mL) smoked paprika
> ½ tsp (2 mL) cayenne pepper
> salt and freshly ground pepper

1. In a large skillet, warm the oil over low heat. Add the onions and cook, stirring regularly, until golden, about 45 minutes.

2. Let cool. Combine with the cream cheese and spices.

NOTE
Rummage through your pantry and try this recipe with whatever you find (preserved garlic, smoked tomatoes, preserved tomatoes, what have you).

On opening night at Garde-Manger, we had no idea what to serve with the bread. Olive oil, butter, we weren't sure. We had a large amount of cream cheese on hand, one of the basic ingredients for our crew meals. One of the kitchen crew decided to add caramelized onions to the cream cheese. And so this spread was born. At Garde-Manger it has become one of our signature staples.

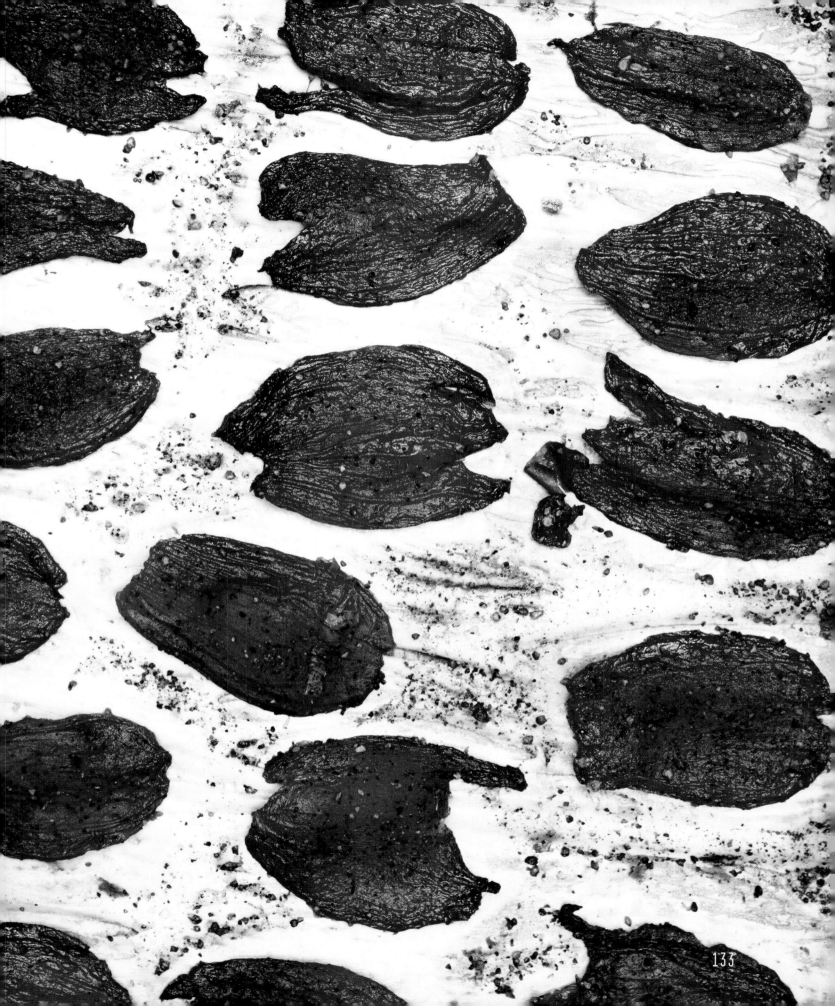

PRESERVED TOMATOES

Prep: 5 min -- Cook: 8 h -- Serves: 4

> **12 Roma tomatoes, blanched, peeled, cut in half lengthwise, and seeded**
> **1 head garlic, cut in half crosswise**
> **2 tbsp (30 mL) olive oil, plus more for storing**
> **leaves from 4 sprigs rosemary, finely chopped**
> **leaves from 4 sprigs thyme, finely chopped**
> **salt and freshly ground pepper**
> **2 tbsp (30 mL) icing sugar**

1. Preheat the oven to 200°F (100°C).

2. Spread the tomatoes, cut side down, on a parchment-lined baking sheet. Add the garlic. Drizzle with olive oil, then sprinkle the herbs over top. Season with salt and pepper. Using a fine sieve, sift the icing sugar over the tomatoes. Cook in the oven overnight or until the tomatoes are softened and wrinkled.

3. Let cool. Transfer the tomatoes to jars, cover with olive oil, and store in the fridge. They will keep for a couple of weeks.

NOTE
Use only the very best ripe tomatoes. If you are short on time and cooking overnight is not an option, roast the tomatoes at 400°F (200°C) for 45 minutes. The flavours will be less intense but just as good.

SMOKED TOMATO VINAIGRETTE

Prep: 15 min -- Cook: 15 min -- Makes: 4 cups (1 L)

> 12 vine-ripened tomatoes, cut in half crosswise and seeded
> 1 shallot, thinly sliced
> leaves from 2 sprigs tarragon
> 1 cup (250 mL) olive oil
> 1 tbsp (15 mL) honey
> juice of ½ lemon
> salt and freshly ground pepper

Smoke the tomatoes, shallot, and tarragon in a smoker for 15 minutes. Coarsely purée the mixture in a blender. Stir in the olive oil, honey, and lemon juice. Season with salt and pepper.

NOTE

A smoker really is a good investment. It adds a lot of flavour and is not expensive. If you don't have access to one, use preserved tomatoes (see recipe p. 134). Add the shallot and tarragon when you are ready to purée.

FISH AND SEAFOOD

FISH AND SEAFOOD

--

Fish and seafood are prominent at Garde-Manger, as they are an indulgence of mine. I absolutely love them. With each new shipment of octopus, crab, shrimp, grouper, sea urchins, clams, periwinkles, or oysters, there are innumerable creative culinary possibilities. Seafood is "feast food" to me: not only do you get to eat with your fingers, but you can get as messy as you want as well!

Long live the lobster and all manner of seafood!

PAN-COOKED SMOKED SALMON WITH CRÈME FRAÎCHE AND FENNEL SALAD

Prep: 10 min -- Cook: 1 min -- Serves: 4

At Garde-Manger we buy a whole side of lightly smoked salmon, skin on, and cut it into fillets or chunks ourselves. Of course you can smoke your own if you're adventurous! This salad is meant to be served with the salmon barely warmed through, the skin a little bit crispy. It's a great combination of textures and temperatures.

FENNEL SALAD
> 1 English cucumber, peeled
> 1 fennel bulb, grated
> 1 handful chopped chives
> 1 handful chopped dill
> 2 tbsp (30 mL) olive oil
> 1 tbsp (15 mL) white balsamic vinegar
> juice of 1 lemon
> salt and freshly ground pepper
> 2 tbsp (30 mL) trout caviar (roe)
> ¼ cup (60 mL) crème fraîche (see below)

PAN-COOKED SMOKED SALMON
> 1 tbsp (15 mL) canola oil
> 4 fillets smoked salmon, skin on

For the fennel salad:
1. Coarsely grate the cucumber and squeeze out some of the liquid. Add the fennel, chives, and dill.

2. In a small bowl, whisk the olive oil with the vinegar and lemon juice until emulsified. Season with salt and pepper. Pour over the fennel mixture and toss.

For the pan-cooked smoked salmon:
3. In a small skillet, heat the oil over high heat. Cook the salmon, skin side down, for 1 minute, until the skin is golden and crispy.

4. Divide the salad among 4 plates, top each with a piece of smoked salmon, and garnish with the trout caviar and crème fraîche.

CRÈME FRAÎCHE

Prep: 1 min -- Standing time: 24 h -- Makes: 2 cups (500 mL)

> 2 cups (500 mL) 35% cream
> 3½ tbsp (50 mL) buttermilk

Combine and let sit, covered at room temperature, for 24 hours or until thickened.

LOBSTER POACHED IN BUTTER WITH PRESERVED DUCK AND LOBSTER MUSHROOMS

Prep: 30 min -- Cook: 30 min -- Serves: 4

One of the richest dishes on our menu: unbelievably decadent!

ROASTED LEEKS
> 1 tbsp (15 mL) olive oil
> 4 leeks (white and pale green parts only), cut in half lengthwise
> salt and freshly ground pepper

LOBSTER POACHED IN BUTTER
> 2 lobsters, each 1½ lb (675 g)
> 1 lb (450 g) butter

LOBSTER MUSHROOMS AND FINGERLING POTATOES
> 2 tbsp (30 mL) olive oil
> ½ lb (225 g) fingerling potatoes, boiled and cut in half lengthwise
> ½ lb (225 g) lobster mushrooms, cut in half
> 1 cup (250 mL) veal stock reduction (see recipe p. 184)
> salt and freshly ground pepper
> 1 handful chopped flat-leaf parsley
> 1 handful chopped chives

GARNISHES
> 4 slices duck foie gras
> salt and freshly ground pepper
> 2 preserved duck legs (see preserved pork belly recipe p. 62 or use store-bought), shredded
> chopped flat-leaf parsley
> chopped chives

For the roasted leeks:
1. Preheat the oven to 350°F (180°C).

2. In a large ovenproof skillet, heat the oil over medium-high heat and cook the leeks on all sides until lightly speckled brown. Season with salt and pepper. Transfer the pan to the oven and roast until the leeks are soft, about 30 minutes.

For the lobster poached in butter:
3. Meanwhile, in a pot of boiling salted water, cook the lobsters for 1½ minutes. Transfer to a bowl of ice water to stop them from cooking further. When they're cool enough to handle, shell them and remove the meat. Reserve any roe. (Keep the shells if you would like to make the lobster stock on p. 105.)

4. In a saucepan, melt the butter over low heat. Poach the lobster meat with any roe for 5 minutes.

For the lobster mushrooms and fingerling potatoes:
5. In a large skillet, heat the oil over medium-high heat. Add the potatoes, cut side down, and brown the cut side. Add the mushrooms and sauté until browned. Add the veal stock and continue cooking for a few minutes to heat through. Season with salt and pepper. Add the parsley and chives. Remove from heat and keep warm.

6. Season the slices of foie gras with salt and pepper. In a very hot cast-iron pan, cook the foie gras for 30 seconds on each side.

7. Divide the leeks among 4 plates. Add the mushrooms and potatoes, the shredded duck, the poached lobster, and a slice of foie gras. Garnish with parsley and chives.

NOTE
Adding any lobster roe to the butter for poaching adds both colour and flavour.

CRABOCADO

Prep: 5 min -- Cook: 5 min -- Serves: 4

> 2 avocados
> juice of 2 lemons
> 1 lb (450 g) crab meat
> ½ lb (225 g) asparagus, blanched and coarsely chopped
> 2 tbsp (30 mL) chopped chives
> 2 tbsp (30 mL) chopped flat-leaf parsley
> 1 tbsp (15 mL) chopped dill
> 1 tbsp (15 mL) seasoned sour cream (see recipe p. 98)
> ½ tsp (2 mL) jerk seasoning
> 8 large steak spice croutons (see recipe p. 100), crushed
> Maldon sea salt and freshly ground pepper

1. Peel and slice the avocados. Pour the lemon juice over the avocados so they do not brown. Arrange them on 4 plates.

2. In a bowl, combine the crab meat, asparagus, chives, parsley, dill, seasoned sour cream, jerk seasoning, and crushed croutons. Mix well, then season with Maldon salt and freshly ground pepper. Top the avocados with this mixture.

NOTE

Depending on the season, you can use green beans or other vegetables in place of the asparagus.

PAN-ROASTED HALIBUT WITH GARDEN TOMATOES

Prep: 10 min -- Cook: 10 min -- Serves: 4

This is a seasonal recipe, all about fresh, simple ingredients. We only serve it in summer when the tomatoes are incredibly sweet.

ROASTED VEGETABLES
- > **12 mini zucchini or mini squash**
- > **12 heirloom cherry tomatoes, with stems**
- > **salt and freshly ground pepper**
- > **3 tbsp (45 mL) olive oil**
- > **¼ cup (60 mL) chopped dill**

PAN-ROASTED HALIBUT
- > **3 tbsp (45 mL) olive oil**
- > **4 thick skin-on halibut fillets**
- > **salt and freshly ground pepper**

For the roasted vegetables:
1. Preheat the oven to 400°F (200°C).

2. Spread the zucchini and tomatoes on a baking sheet. Sprinkle with salt and pepper and drizzle with olive oil. Roast for about 10 minutes or until beginning to soften.

For the pan-roasted halibut:
3. While the vegetables are roasting, heat the oil in a large skillet over medium-high heat. Season the halibut with salt and pepper and cook, skin side down, about 5 minutes, until crispy and golden. Turn the fish over and continue cooking for 5 minutes or until tender and flaky.

4. Serve the halibut on a bed of zucchini and tomatoes, garnished with the dill.

NOTE
Mme Guylaine Martin of the Jardinet de la Paysanne, in St-Samuel-de-Horton near Victoriaville, supplies us with our magnificent mini vegetables.

146

OYSTERS WITH BACON AND PARMESAN

Prep: 10 min -- Cook: 15 min -- Serves: 4 to 8

I call these and the oysters Rockefeller (p. 150) "oysters for beginners." They are utterly delicious—but if you're like me, you take your oysters raw and briny.

> ¼ cup (60 mL) 35% cream
> 48 fresh oysters
> 1 shallot, finely chopped
> 1 tbsp (15 mL) olive oil
> 1 tsp (5 mL) Dijon mustard
> 1 cup (250 mL) grated Parmigiano-Reggiano
> freshly ground pepper
> 4 thick slices bacon, diced
> 2 tbsp (30 mL) butter
> ½ cup (125 mL) fresh bread crumbs
> coarse salt
> 1 handful thinly sliced chives
> 1 handful finely chopped flat-leaf parsley (optional)

1. In a small saucepan, reduce the cream by half.

2. Meanwhile, working over a fine sieve set over a large saucepan, shuck the oysters. Put the oysters in the pot. Set aside the rounded bottom half of the shells. Poach the oysters in their liquor for 30 seconds, until firm.

3. Remove the oysters from the pot and set aside in a bowl. Reduce the oyster liquor by half. Add to the reduced cream.

4. In another small saucepan, sauté the shallot in the olive oil until translucent. Add the cream mixture, Dijon mustard, and half the Parmesan. Season with pepper. Set aside and keep warm.

5. Preheat the broiler.

6. In a skillet on high heat, sauté the diced bacon until golden and crisp. Drain on paper towels.

7. Add the butter to the skillet, then cook the bread crumbs over medium-high heat until golden.

8. Spread some coarse salt in a baking dish and place the oyster shells on the salt. Place an oyster in each shell. Top with the bacon, cream sauce, bread crumbs, and the remaining Parmesan. Broil for a couple of minutes, to melt the cheese. Garnish with the chives and parsley and serve.

NOTE

Oysters are naturally salty. Season only if necessary and only when just about to serve.

I am first and foremost an oyster lover. I love shucking them and I love eating them! East Coast oysters—I love them all, with their pros and cons.

OYSTERS ROCKEFELLER

Prep: 10 min -- Cook: 15 min -- Serves: 4 to 8

- > **2 cups (500 mL) 35% cream**
- > **48 fresh oysters**
- > **1 tbsp (15 mL) Dijon mustard**
- > **¼ cup (60 mL) grated Parmigiano-Reggiano**
- > **1 lb (450 g) fresh spinach**
- > **2 tbsp (30 mL) butter**
- > **½ cup (125 mL) fresh bread crumbs**
- > **coarse salt**
- > **freshly ground pepper**

1. In a saucepan, reduce the cream by half.

2. Meanwhile, working over a fine sieve set over a large saucepan, shuck the oysters. Put the oysters in the pot. Set aside the rounded bottom half of the shells. Poach the oysters in their liquor for 30 seconds, until firm.

3. Remove the oysters from the pot and set aside in a bowl. Reduce the oyster liquor by half. Add the reduced cream, Dijon mustard, and half the Parmesan. Set aside.

4. In a skillet over low heat, cook the spinach in a bit of water for a few minutes until it is wilted. Wring the water out of the spinach, chop the spinach finely, and add it to the cream mixture.

5. In the same skillet over medium-high heat, melt the butter. Cook the bread crumbs until golden.

6. Preheat the broiler.

7. Spread some coarse salt in the bottom of a baking dish and place the oysters shells on the salt. Place an oyster in each shell. Top with the creamed spinach, the bread crumbs, and the remaining Parmesan. Broil for a couple of minutes, to melt the cheese. Finish with a grinding of pepper.

NOTE

Oysters are naturally salty. Season only if necessary and only when just about to serve.

Instead of Parmesan, you can use a blend of Emmental and Gruyère or an aged Cheddar.

You can serve 2 oysters per shell if you like.

150

SEA URCHINS AND POACHED EGGS

Prep: 5 min -- Cook: 2 min -- Serves: 4

Occasionally, sea urchin comes our way. Its delicate flavour goes beautifully with gently poached egg yolk.

> **4 sea urchins**
> **4 egg yolks**
> **fresh seaweed**
> **finely chopped chives**
> **Maldon sea salt and freshly ground pepper**

1. Using scissors, cut away about a third of the sea urchin shell to make a circular opening in the top. Delicately remove the coral (the roe) and set aside. Clean the shells. Put the coral back in the shells. Carefully place an egg yolk in each.

2. Cover the bottom of a casserole dish with the seaweed. Put the shells on top. Pour a little water over the seaweed. Bring to a rolling boil, cover, and cook for 2 minutes.

3. Garnish with chives, Maldon salt, and pepper. Serve with toasted brioche.

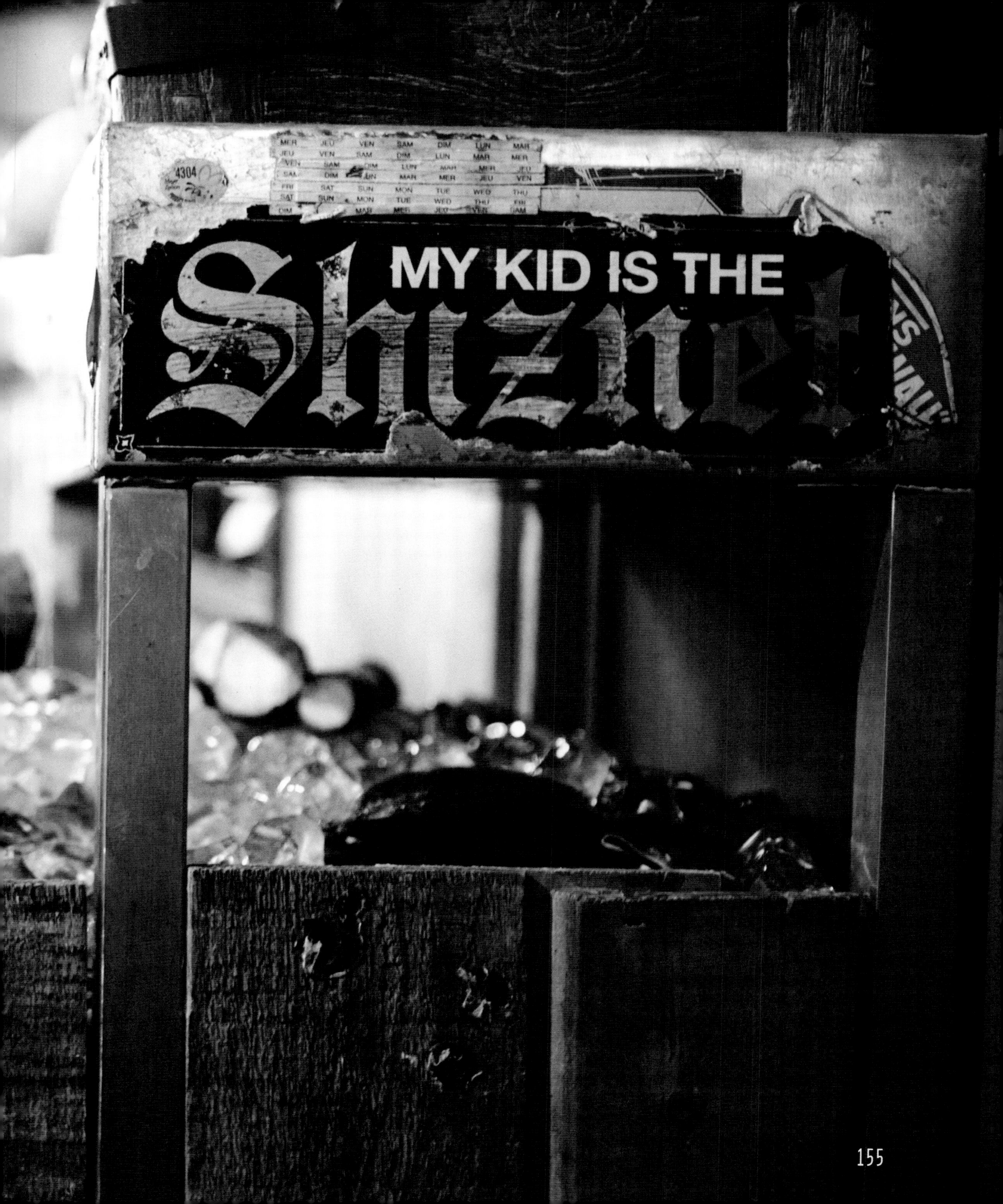
MY KID IS THE
4304

SALMON TARTARE

Prep: 10 min -- Serves: 4

Of course, use only the freshest salmon for this recipe. Buy it from a trusted fishmonger and keep the fish as cold as possible. We like to use bigger cubes, as they give better texture. Get creative with herbs and seasonings and put your own stamp on this easy, great dish.

> 1 lb (450 g) freshest salmon, cut in cubes
> 3 tbsp (45 mL) capers
> 4 vine-ripened tomatoes, seeded and diced
> 6 asparagus spears, blanched and diced
> 12 steak spice croutons (see recipe p. 100)
> 1 handful thinly sliced chives
> 1 handful finely chopped parsley
> 1 handful chopped celery leaves
> 2 tbsp (30 mL) olive oil
> couple of drops green Tabasco sauce, to taste
> salt and freshly ground pepper
> 1 tbsp (15 mL) grated fresh horseradish
> zest of 1 lemon

In a large bowl, combine the salmon, capers, tomatoes, asparagus, croutons, chives, parsley, celery leaves, olive oil, and Tabasco. Toss well. Season with salt and pepper. Spoon onto plates. Garnish with fresh horseradish and lemon zest.

PAN-COOKED TROUT WITH SAUTÉED LETTUCE AND MASHED AVOCADO

Prep: 30 min -- Cook: 10 min -- Serves: 4

This recipe could not be simpler. A little bit of lemon, a bunch of fresh parsley, and a super-hot pan add up to a fantastic dish.

MASHED AVOCADO
> 2 avocados
> finely chopped parsley, to taste
> juice of ½ lemon
> couple of drops green Tabasco sauce
> salt and freshly ground pepper

PAN-COOKED TROUT
> 2 tbsp (30 mL) olive oil
> 4 skin-on trout fillets
> salt and freshly ground pepper
> zest and juice of 1 lemon
> 2 tbsp (30 mL) butter
> chopped dill, to taste

SAUTÉED LETTUCE
> 2 tbsp (30 mL) butter
> 1 shallot, thinly sliced
> 4 cups (1 L) coarsely chopped rice lettuce, romaine, or bibb lettuce
> salt and freshly ground pepper

For the avocado:
1. Coarsely mash the avocados with a fork. Add the remaining ingredients and set aside.

For the pan-cooked trout:
2. Heat the oil in a large skillet on high heat. Season the trout fillets with salt and pepper. Cook the fillets, skin side down, about 5 minutes, until golden and crispy. Transfer the fillets to a plate and keep warm. Wipe any excess oil from the pan with a paper towel. Reduce the heat to medium and deglaze the pan with the lemon juice. Add the lemon zest, then whisk in the butter. Add the dill and set aside.

For the sautéed lettuce:
3. Melt the butter in a large skillet over medium-high heat. Sauté the shallot until it softens but isn't browning. Add the lettuce and sauté until it wilts, about 3 minutes. Season with salt and pepper.

4. Spoon a bed of mashed avocado on each plate. Top with a trout fillet. Top with the sautéed lettuce and a drizzle of the lemon-butter pan sauce.

NOTE
Rice lettuce can be hard to find. It tastes somewhat like romaine, but it is softer and more delicate.

It is not necessary to turn the trout and cook it on the other side. Residual heat will cook it through. Serve pink.

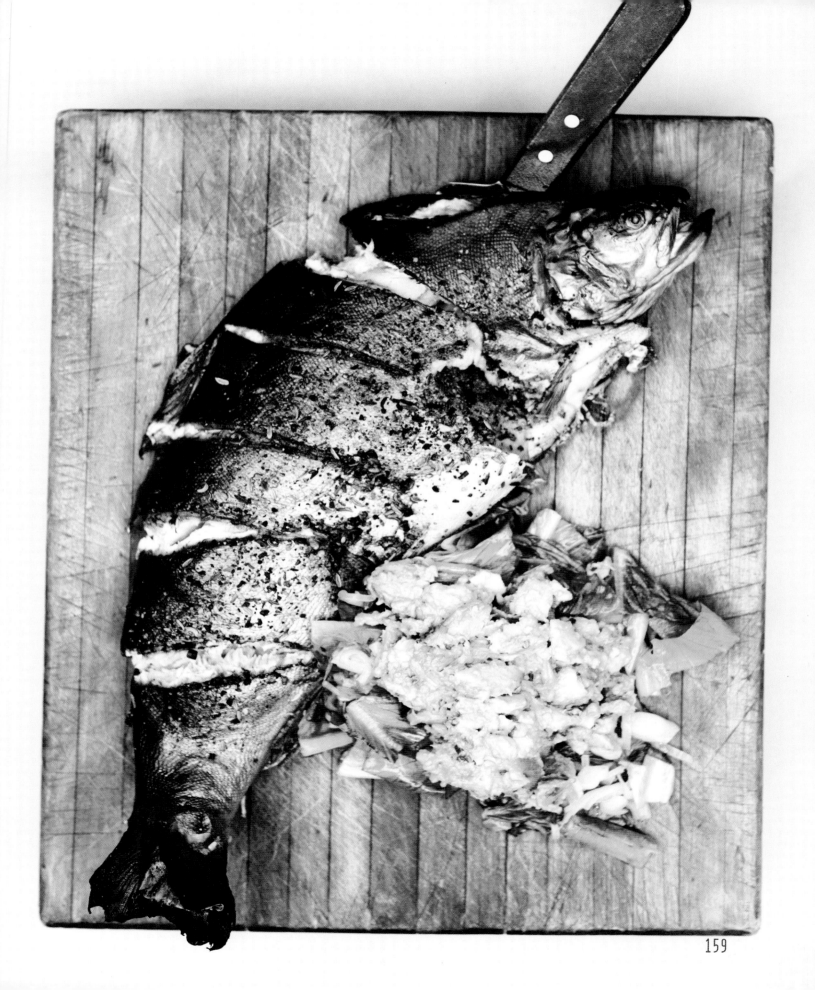

POTATO CRAZY

POTATO CRAZY

--

Potatoes are like a blank canvas to me—
you can paint them any way you want.

A mound of mashed potatoes can cradle all manner
of goodies in its spooned-out crater, from the
simplest to the most refined ingredients. With lobster
in lobster sauce or mashed with roasted garlic and
fresh goat cheese, potatoes are versatile and user
friendly. With potatoes, creativity knows no bounds.

THE "HOW TO" FOR MASHED POTATOES

We always have large quantities of boiled potatoes on hand at the restaurant, at least three days' worth. We always boil them skin on for extra flavour. They are kept in the fridge, barely mashed, no seasonings added.

When we're ready to serve, we heat butter and cream in a pan, then gradually add the potatoes to heat them through. We then mash this mixture. Any remaining ingredients are always added at the very end.

TINBITS

Prep: 15 min -- Cook: 5 min -- Serves: 4

Tinbits are delicious little potato doughnuts.

> ¾ cup (175 mL) milk
> ¼ cup (60 mL) butter
> salt and freshly ground pepper
> ¾ cup (175 mL) unbleached flour
> 3 eggs
> 2 Yukon Gold potatoes (unpeeled), boiled and mashed
> ½ lb (225 g) cottage cheese
> canola or peanut oil for deep-frying

1. Bring the milk, butter, and a little salt to a boil in a saucepan. Remove from the heat. Add the flour all at once, stirring vigorously with a wooden spoon until the mixture forms a ball that no longer sticks to the sides of the pot. Put the pot back on medium heat and cook for about 2 minutes, stirring constantly.

2. Let cool for a few minutes. Whisk in the eggs, 1 at a time, until the dough is smooth and shiny and thoroughly mixed. (You could do this with an electric beater.) This is cream-puff dough.

3. Beat the mashed potatoes into the cream-puff dough. Beat in the cottage cheese. Season with salt and pepper.

4. Heat the oil in a deep-fryer or large, deep pot to 350°F (180°C).

5. Roll the dough into little balls. Working in batches, fry until the tinbits are golden and crispy. Drain on paper towels and season with salt and pepper. Serve hot.

NOTE

You can add other ingredients, such as cooked bacon bits or a stronger cheese, blue cheese for instance. Season with cayenne pepper for spicy tinbits. Use corn flour for a totally different consistency.

Serve with Tex-Mex sauce or spicy mayonnaise (see recipe p. 111).

Add tinbits to your favourite recipes. Make some poutine with them and serve with fried hot chicken drumsticks (see recipe p. 68).

POTATOES WITH LOBSTER

Prep: 30 min -- Cook: 30 min -- Serves: 4

LOBSTER
> 2 lobsters, each 1½ lb (675 g)

POTATOES
> 4 Yukon Gold potatoes (unpeeled)
> ½ cup (125 mL) butter, melted
> ½ cup (125 mL) 35% cream, heated
> ¼ cup (60 mL) thinly sliced chives, plus more for garnish
> salt and freshly ground pepper

LOBSTER SAUCE
> 4 cups (1 L) lobster stock (see recipe p. 105)
> 3 tbsp (45 mL) butter, diced
> salt and freshly ground pepper

For the lobster:
1. In a large pot of boiling salted water, cook the lobsters for 6 minutes. Put the lobsters in ice water to stop them from cooking further. When they are cool enough to handle, shell them and set aside the lobster meat. (Keep the shells to make the lobster stock on p. 105.)

For the potatoes:
2. Boil the potatoes, drain them, and coarsely mash them with the butter and cream. Add the chives, salt, and pepper. Set aside and keep warm.

For the lobster sauce:
3. Meanwhile, reduce the lobster stock by half. Whisk in the butter, a little at a time. Season with salt and pepper. Set aside and keep warm.

4. Using an ice cream scoop, put a scoop of mashed potatoes in the centre of each plate. Make a hole in the middle. Put some lobster meat in the hole and top with the lobster sauce. Garnish with the additional chives.

ROASTED GARLIC POTATOES

Prep: 15 min -- Cook: 30 min -- Serves: 4

> 4 Yukon Gold potatoes
  (unpeeled)
> 1 head roasted garlic
  (see recipe p. 96)
> ½ cup (125 mL) 35% cream,
  heated
> ½ cup (125 mL) butter, melted
> ½ cup (125 mL) fresh goat cheese
> salt and freshly ground pepper

1. Boil the potatoes, drain them,
   and coarsely mash them with
   the roasted garlic, cream, and
   butter. Stir in the goat cheese.
   Season with salt and pepper.

POTATOES WITH MARROW

Prep: 15 min -- Cook: 30 min -- Serves: 4

> **6 marrow bones**
> **4 Yukon Gold potatoes (unpeeled)**
> **½ cup (125 mL) butter, melted**
> **½ cup (125 mL) 35% cream, heated**
> **½ cup (125 mL) chopped flat-leaf parsley**
> **salt and freshly ground pepper**

1. Preheat the oven to 350°F (180°C).

2. Place the marrow bones on a baking sheet and roast for about 15 minutes, until the marrow is tender and comes off the bone. Remove the marrow from the bones and set aside.

3. Meanwhile, boil the potatoes, drain them, and coarsely mash them with the butter and cream. Stir in the marrow and parsley. Season with salt and pepper.

NOTE
These potatoes are best served with red meat, but are just as good with chicken. They're excellent in shepherd's pie or pan-fried and topped with an egg . . . too good for words!

POTATO SMASH WITH OLIVE OIL

Prep: 15 min -- Cook: 30 min -- Serves: 4

> **4 Yukon Gold potatoes (unpeeled)**
> **½ cup (125 mL) olive oil**
> **leaves from 4 sprigs thyme, chopped**
> **2 garlic cloves, finely chopped**
> **chopped parsley or dill, to taste**
> **salt and freshly ground pepper**

Boil the potatoes, drain them, and using a wooden spoon, crush them just enough that the potatoes are lumpy, not smooth. Stir in the olive oil, then the remaining ingredients.

NOTE
This dish is called a "smash" because it is lumpy, not smooth.

This smash is lighter than the one we make with butter and cream. It's perfect warm-weather fare, served at room temperature with steamed fish.

Fresh dill is best in this smash when served with smoked mackerel or trout. If serving with something more along the lines of rare filet of bison in peppercorn sauce, chopped parsley is a better choice.

This smash is wonderful with lamb chops, a slice of terrine, tuna, or canned sardines. You might want to serve it with smoked tomato vinaigrette (see recipe p. 135) topped with a fillet of sole.

RÖSTI

Prep: 15 min -- Cook: 30 min -- Serves: 4

> **4 Yukon Gold potatoes (unpeeled)**
> **1 shallot, thinly sliced**
> **4 cloves roasted garlic (see recipe p. 96)**
> **1 egg, beaten**
> **salt and freshly ground pepper**
> **2 tbsp (30 mL) olive oil**
> **2 tbsp (30 mL) butter**

1. Preheat the oven to 400°F (200°C).

2. Boil the potatoes, drain them, and coarsely grate them. Mix the potatoes with the shallot, roasted garlic, and beaten egg. Season with salt and pepper.

3. Flatten the mixture into 4 pancake shapes. In a large ovenproof skillet over medium-high heat, heat the oil and butter. Cook the "pancakes" for a few minutes on each side, until they are crispy and golden. Transfer the pan to the oven for 5 minutes to cook through.

NOTE
Serve with seasoned sour cream (see recipe p. 98) or ricotta, along with preserved tomatoes (see recipe p. 134) and some greens.

FRITES

Prep: 15 min -- Cook: 10 min -- Serves: 4

> **6 Yukon Gold potatoes (unpeeled), cut into fries**
> **canola or peanut oil for deep-frying**
> **salt and freshly ground pepper**

1. Heat the oil in a deep-fryer or large, deep pot to 250°F (120°C).

2. Cook the potatoes for 2 or 3 minutes to blanch them. Strain. (The potatoes can be set aside at this point for up to 2 hours.)

3. Raise the temperature of the oil to 350°F (180°C). Put the frites back into the oil and fry until crispy and golden.

4. Drain on paper towels. Season with salt and pepper.

NOTE
At the restaurant we blanch the potatoes at the beginning of the day, then do the second frying once they're ordered.

You can also use a mandoline to thinly slice the potatoes into chips. Season them with smoked salt.

SMALL PLATES

SMALL PLATES

--

At the end of the night, when all the guests have been served, the kitchen crew are usually famished. So it is our turn to feast! There are plenty of leftovers at Garde-Manger, and with a pinch of creativity and a bowlful of ingredients, we often sit down to a meal fit for a king. Lobster rolls, shrimp rolls, tartares, and crispy shrimp in spiced honey—all make for delicious and easy-to-fix snacks.

SALT COD FRITTERS (ACRAS) WITH JERK MAYONNAISE

Standing time: 3 days -- Prep: 15 min -- Cook: 15 min -- Serves: 4

This grew out of a staff meal I used to have when I worked at a Portuguese restaurant. Add some Jamaican jerk spice and it's a match made in heaven.

- > 1 lb (450 g) boneless salt cod
- > 2 lb (900 g) fresh cod fillets
- > salt and freshly ground pepper
- > 2 tbsp (30 mL) olive oil
- > 4 Yukon Gold potatoes, boiled and mashed
- > ½ cup (125 mL) sour cream
- > 2 shallots, finely chopped
- > 1 fresh red chili pepper, seeded and very finely chopped
- > 1 inch (2.5 cm) fresh ginger, very finely chopped
- > ½ cup (125 mL) chopped chives
- > ½ cup (125 mL) chopped flat-leaf parsley
- > ¼ cup (60 mL) chopped dill
- > 1 tbsp (15 mL) chopped thyme
- > 1 tsp (5 mL) jerk seasoning
- > ½ head roasted garlic (see recipe p. 96)
- > canola or peanut oil for deep-frying
- > 4 egg whites
- > jerk mayonnaise (see recipe p. 111)

1. Put the salt cod in a bowl of cold water and refrigerate it for 3 days, rinsing the fish and changing the water daily. On the third day, drain the fish, rinse it, and press it firmly to remove all excess water. Shred the fish and put it in a large bowl.

2. Season the fresh cod with salt and pepper. Coat it with olive oil. Steam it for 10 minutes. Let cool, shred it, and add it to the salt cod.

3. Add the mashed potatoes, sour cream, shallots, chili pepper, ginger, chives, parsley, dill, thyme, jerk seasoning, and roasted garlic. Mix well.

4. Heat the oil in a deep-fryer or large, deep pot to 375°F (190°C).

5. Beat the egg whites into soft mounds. Delicately fold the egg whites into the cod mixture. Check seasonings. Shape into little balls. Working in batches if necessary, fry for 3 minutes or until the fritters are crispy and golden. Drain on paper towels.

6. Serve with jerk mayonnaise.

NOTE
If you don't like mayo, use sour cream or a mixture of both.

CRAB BLT

Prep: 30 min -- Cook: 10 min -- Serves: 4

One of the highlights of our year is soft-shell crab season. This incredibly tasty, crunchy, savoury sandwich is my favourite way to enjoy these delicate creatures.

FRIED SOFT-SHELL CRABS
> 4 soft-shell crabs
> 2 cups (500 mL) panko bread crumbs
> ¼ cup (60 mL) flour
> ½ tsp (2 mL) cayenne pepper
> salt and freshly ground black pepper
> canola or peanut oil for deep-frying
> 8 eggs

SANDWICHES
> 4 slices country loaf
> ¼ cup (60 mL) spicy mayonnaise (see recipe p. 111)
> 8 slices bacon, cooked to taste
> lettuce leaves (watercress, arugula, iceberg, Boston, etc.)
> 2 tomatoes, sliced
> salt and freshly ground pepper

For the crabs:
1. Cut the head off the crabs with a very sharp knife. Lift the shell and remove the gills. Pull on the tail to remove it. Rinse the crab roe under the faucet.

2. In a food processor, finely grind the panko crumbs. Transfer to a bowl and whisk in the flour, cayenne, and salt and black pepper.

3. Heat the oil in a deep-fryer or large, deep pot to 350°F (180°C).

4. Put the eggs in a bowl and beat them. Dredge the crabs in the panko mixture, then in the beaten eggs, and once again in the panko mixture. Fry them until crispy and golden, about 4 to 5 minutes. Drain on paper towels. Season.

For the sandwiches:
5. Toast the bread. Cut each slice in half. Spread the spicy mayonnaise on half the slices. Put the fried crabs on the other slices and garnish with bacon, lettuce, and tomatoes. Season with salt and pepper. Top with the mayo slice and serve.

NOTE
There are a number of varieties of soft-shell crab at the fishmonger. Actually, the soft shell is due to their age, not their variety. During moulting season, when the crab sheds its old shell and forms a new one, it can be eaten whole (except for the gills, the mouth and eyes, and the viscera). Soft-shell crab is available from May to July. The ever-popular American East Coast blue crab can be found in some Quebec fish markets.

SEARED BEEF WITH BEET SALAD

Prep: 15 min -- Cook: 5 min -- Serves: 4

Not quite carpaccio, this beef is seared very quickly and served "bleu." The beets add an earthy, sweet undertone to this gorgeous dish.

BEET SALAD

> **4 raw beets, peeled and grated**
> **chopped dill, to taste**
> **1 tbsp (15 mL) olive oil**
> **1 tbsp (15 mL) white balsamic vinegar**
> **salt and freshly ground pepper**
> **4 eggs**
> **¼ cup (60 mL) seasoned sour cream (see recipe p. 98)**

SEARED BEEF

> **1 lb (450 g) beef sirloin**
> **salt and freshly ground pepper**
> **2 tbsp (30 mL) steak spices (see recipe p. 101)**
> **2 tbsp (30 mL) canola oil**

For the beet salad:

1. Combine the beets, dill, olive oil, and balsamic vinegar in a bowl. Season with salt and pepper. Set aside.

For the beef:

2. Season the beef with salt and pepper and the steak spices. In a very hot cast-iron pan, heat the oil. Sear the beef on both sides. Set aside.

3. In a pot of boiling salted water, cook the eggs for 6 minutes. Drain, rinse in cold water, and peel.

4. Slice the beef and divide it among 4 plates. Top with the beet salad, and top each serving with a soft-boiled egg. Garnish with the seasoned sour cream.

SHIITAKE MUSHROOM, GOAT CHEESE, AND SPECK BRUSCHETTA

Prep: 15 min -- Cook: 30 min -- Serves: 4

At Garde-Manger we make lots of different versions of what we call bruschetta. They all start with a thick slice of amazing country bread, toasted up with a good dose of olive oil and garlic. You can think of tons of toppings starting off with a great base like that.

VEAL STOCK REDUCTION
> 4 cups (1 L) veal stock (see recipe p. 106 or use store-bought)
> ¼ cup (60 mL) butter, diced
> salt and freshly ground pepper

CROUTONS
> 2 tbsp (30 mL) olive oil
> 2 tbsp (30 mL) butter
> 4 thick slices country loaf
> 4 cloves roasted garlic (see recipe p. 96)
> 1 cup (250 mL) fresh goat cheese

SHIITAKE MUSHROOMS
> 2 tbsp (30 mL) olive oil
> 2 tbsp (30 mL) butter
> ½ lb (225 g) shiitake mushrooms, stemmed
> 1 shallot, finely chopped
> 1 garlic clove, finely chopped
> salt and freshly ground pepper
--
> 4 slices speck, julienned (see Note)

For the veal stock reduction:
1. In a large saucepan, reduce the veal stock by about half. Whisk in the butter, a little at a time. Season with salt and pepper. Set aside and keep warm.

For the croutons:
2. Heat the oil and butter in a large skillet over medium-high heat. Fry the bread until golden on both sides. Spread one side with the roasted garlic. Set aside.

For the shiitake mushrooms:
3. In the same skillet, heat the oil and butter over medium-high heat. Sauté the mushrooms with the shallot and garlic until tender. Season with salt and pepper. Remove from heat.

4. Spread the goat cheese on the croutons. Place in individual soup plates. Spoon the mushrooms onto the croutons, drizzle with some of the veal stock reduction, and garnish with the julienned speck.

NOTE
Speck, like pancetta, guanciale, culatello, and coppa, is part of the family of Italian cured meats called salumi. If you can't find it, use prosciutto, Bayonne ham, or Serrano ham instead.

CLAM CHOWDER

Prep: 35 min -- Cook: 45 min -- Serves: 6 to 8

CHOWDER
> 2 tbsp (30 mL) olive oil, plus more for drizzling
> 6 Yukon Gold potatoes, peeled and chopped
> 1 onion, chopped
> 1 celery rib, chopped
> 6 cups (1.5 L) water
> 2 cups (500 mL) 35% cream
> 1 bay leaf
> salt and freshly ground pepper

CLAMS
> 4 cups (1 L) water
> 4 tbsp (60 mL) butter
> 2 lb (900 g) clams, cleaned
> 4 thick slices bacon, finely diced
> 1 onion, finely diced
> 1 celery rib, finely diced
> 1 Yukon Gold potato, boiled and finely diced
> 1 handful chopped parsley
> 1 handful finely chopped chives
> 1 handful finely chopped dill

TOASTED GARLIC BREAD AU GRATIN
> 4 thick slices country loaf
> 3 tbsp (45 mL) olive oil
> 4 cloves roasted garlic (see recipe p. 96)
> 1 cup (250 mL) grated Emmental or Gruyère cheese

For the chowder:
1. In a large pot, heat the oil over medium-high heat. Sauté the potatoes, onion, and celery until the onion and celery are translucent. Add the water, cream, bay leaf, and salt and pepper. Reduce heat and simmer for 30 minutes or until the vegetables are soft. Remove the bay leaf. Using a food processor or hand blender, purée the chowder until smooth. (For an even smoother texture, press this purée through a sieve.) Return to the pot and set aside.

For the clams:
2. In another large pot over medium-high heat, bring the water and 2 tbsp (30 mL) of the butter to a boil. Add the clams, put the lid on, and cook the clams for 5 minutes or until they open. Strain, reserving the cooking liquid and the clams separately. (Discard any clams that did not open.) Wipe out the pot, and in it brown the bacon in the remaining 2 tbsp (30 mL) butter. Add the onion and celery; cook for 5 minutes or until the vegetables are soft. Add the potato and cook for a couple more minutes. Add the clams and heat through. Stir in the parsley, chives, and dill. Set aside and keep warm.

3. Pour the reserved cooking liquid into the puréed chowder and heat through. Adjust seasoning.

For the toasted garlic bread:
4. While the chowder heats, preheat the broiler. In a large skillet, pan-toast the bread in the olive oil. Spread with the roasted garlic. Top with the Emmental and broil until the cheese melts. Ladle the chowder into individual soup bowls. Add the clam mixture. Drizzle with olive oil. Serve with the toasted garlic bread.

CRISPY SHRIMP IN SPICED HONEY

Prep: 15 min -- Cook: 10 min -- Serves: 4

Sweet, salty, crispy, with a hit of spice: four elements that make a dish addictive.

SPICED HONEY
> 1¼ cups (300 mL) honey
> 1 tbsp (15 mL) ground ginger
> 1 tsp (5 mL) smoked paprika
> ½ tsp (2 mL) hot pepper flakes
> ½ tsp (2 mL) cayenne pepper
> 1 garlic clove
> juice of 1 lime

SHRIMP
> canola or peanut oil for deep-frying
> 2 cups (500 mL) panko bread crumbs
> ½ cup (125 mL) flour
> salt and freshly ground pepper
> 2 lb (900 g) rock shrimp, peeled and deveined
> lemon wedges, for garnish

For the spiced honey:
1. In a small saucepan, bring all the ingredients for the spiced honey to a boil. Turn the heat off and let sit for 15 minutes. Strain through a fine sieve and set aside.

For the shrimp:
2. Heat the oil in a deep-fryer or large, deep pot to 350°F (180°C).

3. In a bowl combine the panko, flour, and salt and pepper. Coat the shrimp in the flour mixture, shaking off any excess. Fry for 2 minutes or until golden and crispy. Drain on paper towels and season with salt and pepper.

4. Serve the shrimp drizzled with the spiced honey, with lemon wedges on the side.

NOTE
Add a little spiced honey to mayonnaise and serve it with fried chicken.

187

LOBSTER ROLL

Prep: 10 min -- Cook: 10 min -- Serves: 4

When I was a kid, we used to spend time in Maine during the summers. This is my ultimate summertime comfort food.

> **4 lobsters, each 1½ lb (675 g), bigger if you like**
> **2 tbsp (30 mL) basic mayonnaise (see recipe p. 111)**
> **2 green onions, finely chopped**
> **salt and freshly ground pepper**
> **lobster butter (see recipe p. 98)**
> **4 hot dog buns**

1. Cook the lobsters for 6 minutes in a large pot of boiling salted water. Submerge them in ice water to stop them from cooking further. When they're cool enough to handle, remove the shells and coarsely chop the lobster meat. (Save the shells for making the lobster stock on p. 105.) Combine the meat with the mayonnaise and green onions. Season with salt and pepper.

2. Spread the lobster butter inside the hot dog buns and toast them on both sides in a skillet. Fill the toasted buns with the lobster mixture and serve.

NOTE
Lobster meat is flavourful and stands on its own. It does not need much seasoning. Keep it simple.

GREEN SALAD WITH PRALINE PECANS

Prep: 10 min -- Cook: 5 min -- Serves: 4

VINAIGRETTE
> 2 tbsp (30 mL) balsamic vinegar
> 1 tbsp (15 mL) maple syrup
> 1 tsp (5 mL) Dijon mustard
> ½ cup (125 mL) canola oil
> salt and freshly ground pepper

SALAD
> ½ lb (225 g) asparagus, blanched and cut in half
> ½ lb (225 g) green beans, blanched
> 1 or 2 cucumbers, seeded and cut in sticks
> 4 endives, shredded
> salt and freshly ground pepper
--
> 1 cup (250 mL) coarsely chopped praline pecans (see recipe p. 114)

For the vinaigrette:
1. Whisk together the balsamic vinegar, maple syrup, and Dijon mustard. Then whisk in the oil until emulsified. Season with salt and pepper.

For the salad:
2. Combine the salad ingredients in a bowl. Add the vinaigrette and toss. Season with salt and pepper. Serve garnished with praline pecans.

NOTE
You can use baby chicory or thinly sliced fennel instead of the endive.

SHRIMP ROLL

Prep: 10 min -- Cook: 5 min -- Serves: 4

> 1 lemon, cut in half
> 2 tbsp (30 mL) Tabasco sauce
> 8 black tiger shrimp, peeled and deveined
> ¼ cup (60 mL) spicy mayonnaise (see recipe p. 111)
> 12 marinated jalapeño pepper slices (see recipe p. 114)
> 2 green onions, finely chopped
> ¼ cup (60 mL) lobster butter (see recipe p. 98)
> 4 hot dog buns
> ¼ cup (60 mL) trout caviar (roe)

1. Squeeze the juice of the lemon into a large pot of boiling salted water, then add the squeezed lemons and the Tabasco sauce. Add the shrimp and cook for 2 minutes. Transfer them to ice water to stop them from cooking further.

2. Drain the shrimp and pat dry. Mix them with the spicy mayonnaise, jalapeño slices, and green onions.

3. Spread the lobster butter inside the hot dog buns and toast them on both sides in a skillet. Fill the toasted buns with the shrimp mixture and garnish with trout caviar.

NOTE

Use a larger number of shrimp if you're cooking smaller ones.

Trout caviar is available just about everywhere. It's very flavourful, smaller than salmon caviar, and very affordable.

Store-bought mayonnaise is all right if you doctor it with lemon juice, cayenne pepper, and a bit of red wine vinegar.

DESSERTS

DESSERTS

--

Desserts are often the crowning glory of a good meal, a pinnacle of tastes that leaves us with unforgettable memories. At Garde-Manger, desserts are also about rediscovering the sweet treats of childhood, the simple comforting tastes that Mom made. My mother is the author of our desserts here at Garde-Manger. On the night before we opened, Mom baked a bunch of pecan pies. At the end of the meal, we placed a whole hot pecan pie on each and every table, to the delight of our guests.

FRIED MARS BARS

Prep: 5 min -- Cook: 2 min -- Serves: 4

This is a Garde-Manger classic. What can I say? My roots are Scottish, and I thought it would be fun to put these on the menu as a little joke. Now I can't take them off—they're always in season!

> **canola or peanut oil for deep-frying**
> **1¼ cups (300 mL) beer**
> **1 cup (250 mL) flour**
> **4 regular-size Mars bars**

1. Heat the oil in a deep-fryer or large, deep pot to 350°F (180°C).

2. In a bowl, whisk together the beer and flour. Coat the Mars bars with the batter. Fry for just 2 or 3 minutes, until the outside is crispy. Drain on paper towels.

3. Serve with vanilla ice cream.

PECAN AND MAPLE BISCOTTI

Prep: 15 min -- Cook: 45 min -- Makes: 12 large biscotti

Fantastic with coffee, these easy biscotti are a great accompaniment to creamy desserts or fruit salad.

> 1 cup (250 mL) maple sugar
> 1 cup (250 mL) flour
> 1 tsp (5 mL) baking powder
> pinch salt
> ½ cup (125 mL) cold butter, diced
> 1 tsp (5 mL) vanilla
> 1 egg
> 1 cup (250 mL) pecans, toasted

1. Preheat the oven to 350°F (180°C).

2. In a food processor, combine the maple sugar, flour, baking powder, and salt. Pulse to combine. Add the diced butter and pulse until crumbly. Add the vanilla and the egg. Pulse just enough to mix lightly.

3. Transfer the dough to a bowl, add the pecans, and work them in with your hands.

4. On a lightly floured surface, press the dough into a 12-inch (30 cm) roll. Put the roll on a parchment-lined baking sheet. Bake for 30 minutes.

5. Transfer to a cutting board and let cool for about 10 minutes. (Do not turn off the oven.) With a sharp bread knife, cut diagonally into ¾-inch (2 cm) slices.

6. Put the biscotti back on the baking sheet, cut side down, and continue baking for about 15 minutes or until crunchy. Transfer biscotti to a rack and let cool.

NOTE

Pistachios, macadamia nuts, and walnuts are good too. You can also add dried cherries or other dried fruit, chocolate chips, orange peel, etc.

MOLASSES COOKIES

Prep: 25 min -- Cook: 20 min -- Makes: 6 to 8 cookies

MOLASSES COOKIES
> 1½ cups (375 mL) butter, softened
> 1 cup (250 mL) brown sugar
> 1 cup (250 mL) molasses
> 2 eggs
> 2 cups (500 mL) flour
> 1 tsp (5 mL) baking powder
> ½ tsp (2 mL) salt

CARAMEL BUTTER
> 1 cup (250 mL) sugar
> 2 tbsp (30 mL) water
> ¼ cup (60 mL) butter, diced
> ¼ cup (60 mL) 35% cream

For the molasses cookies:
1. Preheat the oven to 350°F (180°C). Line a baking sheet with parchment paper, and butter the paper.

2. In a large bowl, beat together the butter and brown sugar until light and fluffy. Beat in the molasses. Add the eggs and continue beating until the mixture thickens.

3. Combine the flour, baking powder, and salt. Add to the molasses mixture and beat just until combined.

4. Pour the batter into the baking sheet and spread it evenly. Bake for 20 minutes or until a toothpick inserted in the middle comes out clean. Let cool.

5. Cut into squares, rectangles, or circles with a cookie cutter.

For the caramel butter:
6. In a small saucepan heat the sugar and water over medium-low heat, stirring with a fork until the sugar dissolves. Continue to cook, swirling the pan from time to time, until it browns lightly. Take the pan off the burner and add the butter, stirring constantly until it becomes caramel. Fold in the cream.

7. Serve the molasses cookies with vanilla ice cream, the caramel butter, and praline pecans (see recipe p. 114).

ROCKY ROAD BROWNIES

Prep: 20 min -- Cook: 45 min -- Makes: 20 brownies

BROWNIES

> 1 cup (250 mL) finely chopped dark chocolate
> ½ cup (125 mL) butter
> 4 eggs
> ½ cup (125 mL) brown sugar
> ½ cup (125 mL) white sugar
> 2 tsp (10 mL) vanilla
> 1 cup (250 mL) flour
> ½ tsp (2 mL) baking powder

GANACHE

> ½ cup (125 mL) finely chopped dark chocolate
> ½ cup (125 mL) 35% cream
> 2 tbsp (30 mL) butter, softened
--
> 10 marshmallows, quartered
> 1 cup (250 mL) hazelnuts, toasted and coarsely chopped

For the brownies:

1. Preheat the oven to 350°F (180°C). Butter a 13- x 9-inch (33 x 23 cm) cake pan and line it with parchment paper.

2. In a small saucepan over low heat, melt the chocolate and the butter, stirring until smooth.

3. In a large bowl, beat the eggs with the brown sugar, white sugar, and vanilla for about 8 minutes, until the mixture is pale and thick. Beat in the flour, baking powder, and chocolate mixture.

4. Pour into the cake pan. Bake for 40 minutes or until the cake is firm and crusty.

For the ganache:

5. In the meantime, put the chopped chocolate in a small bowl. Bring the cream to a boil. Pour it over the chocolate and stir until smooth. Add the butter and stir until combined. Set aside.

6. After the cake has baked for 40 minutes, spread the quartered marshmallows on it and bake for 5 more minutes. Remove from the oven. Sprinkle with the hazelnuts and pour the ganache evenly over the cake. Let cool in the baking dish.

7. Serve with ice cream.

FRUIT CRUMBLE

Prep: 15 min -- Cook: 50 min -- Serves: 6 to 8

This is a go-to dessert for seasonal fruits. Peaches, blueberries, and raspberries are also great here. I know that cornflakes aren't exactly haute cuisine, but neither is this homey, delicious dish. I use the cereal for extra crunchiness. No worries if you don't like it, just leave it out.

CRUMBLE
> 1 cup (250 mL) large-flake rolled oats
> 1 cup (250 mL) crushed cornflakes
> ½ cup (125 mL) unbleached flour
> ½ cup (125 mL) brown sugar
> ¼ cup (60 mL) butter, softened

APPLES
> 8 apples, peeled and sliced medium-thick
> 1 tbsp (15 mL) lemon juice
> ½ cup (125 mL) brown sugar
> ½ tsp (2 mL) cinnamon

1. Preheat the oven to 350°F (180°C).

For the crumble:
2. Whisk together the oats, cornflakes, flour, and brown sugar. Cut in the butter until the mixture resembles coarse crumbs.

For the apples:
3. In a large bowl, toss the apples with the lemon juice. Add the brown sugar and cinnamon; toss to coat thoroughly.

4. Spread the apple mixture in a baking dish. Cover with the crumble mix. Bake for 50 minutes or until the apples are bubbling and tender and the topping is golden.

5. Serve warm or at room temperature with vanilla ice cream.

LEMON AND GRANOLA PARFAIT

Prep: 10 min -- Refrigerate: 4 h -- Cook: 20 min -- Serves: 4

So good. I use cornflakes (or rice cereal) in granola for the crunchiness. It's optional.

STRAINED YOGURT
> 2 cups (500 mL) plain yogurt
> zest of 1 lemon

LEMON CREAM
> 3 eggs
> ½ cup (125 mL) sugar
> zest and juice of 2 lemons
> 1/3 cup (75 mL) cold butter, diced

GRANOLA
> 1 cup (250 mL) large-flake rolled oats
> 1 cup (250 mL) cornflakes
> 1 cup (250 mL) coarsely chopped pecans
> ½ cup (125 mL) dried cherries
> ½ cup (125 mL) honey
> 2 tbsp (30 mL) hazelnut oil
> 1 tsp (5 mL) vanilla

For the strained yogurt:
1. Line a sieve with a paper towel and set it over a bowl. Pour the yogurt into the sieve and refrigerate for 4 hours. Discard the liquid in the bowl. Turn the strained yogurt into the bowl and stir in the lemon zest. Return to the fridge until ready to serve.

For the lemon cream:
2. Combine all the ingredients in a small saucepan. Bring to a boil, stirring. Immediately reduce the heat and simmer, stirring constantly, for 2 minutes, until the cream thickens. Immediately transfer to a bowl and cover the surface of the lemon cream with plastic wrap. Let cool, then chill.

For the granola:
3. Preheat the oven to 350°F (180°C).

4. In a medium bowl, stir together the oats, cornflakes, pecans, and dried cherries. In a small saucepan, bring the honey and oil to a boil. Remove from heat and add the vanilla. Pour over the granola and mix thoroughly.

5. Spread the granola mixture on a parchment-lined baking sheet. Bake for 20 minutes, stirring often to ensure the mixture browns evenly. Let cool.

6. To serve, spoon the yogurt into serving glasses. Top with the lemon cream, then top with a spoonful or two of the granola.

ICE CREAM SANDWICHES

Prep: 15 min -- Cook: 10 min -- Makes: 24 large cookies

> 1½ cups (375 mL) brown sugar
> 1 cup (250 mL) butter, melted
> 3 eggs
> 1 tsp (5 mL) vanilla
> 1¾ cups (425 mL) flour
> 1 tsp (5 mL) baking soda
> pinch salt
> 2½ cups (625 mL) large-flake rolled oats
> 1½ cups (375 mL) finely chopped chocolate
> ice cream, any flavour you like

1. Preheat the oven to 350°F (180°C).

2. In a bowl, whisk the brown sugar into the melted butter. Add the eggs and vanilla and whisk until everything is nicely blended.

3. In another bowl, whisk together the flour, baking soda, and salt. Stir into the brown sugar mixture, then blend in the oats and chocolate.

4. Place 12 large spoonfuls of the cookie dough on a greased baking sheet. Bake for 10 minutes or until the cookies are lightly browned.

5. Let them cool a bit and then make ice cream sandwiches with them.

NOTE
You can always skip the ice cream and eat the cookies straight from the oven. They're wonderful!

STRAWBERRY SHORTCAKE

Prep: 30 min -- Cook: 25 min -- Macerate: 1 h -- Serves: 4

Quebec strawberries are second to none. This shortcake is a fantastic showcase for them.

GÉNOISE (SPONGE CAKE)
> 6 eggs
> ½ cup (125 mL) sugar
> 1 tsp (5 mL) vanilla
> 1 cup (250 mL) flour
> ½ cup (125 mL) butter, melted

MASHED STRAWBERRIES
> 2 cups (500 mL) strawberries, hulled and cut in half
> ¼ cup (60 mL) sugar
> 1 vanilla bean, cut in half lengthwise

SWEET CREAM CHEESE
> 1 lb (450 g) cream cheese, softened
> ½ cup (125 mL) icing sugar
> 2 tbsp (30 mL) 35% cream

GARNISH
> fresh strawberries, cut in half

For the génoise:
1. Preheat the oven to 350°F (180°C). Butter the sides of a 17- x 11-inch (45 x 29 cm) baking sheet and line it with parchment paper, leaving an overhang on each side.

2. In a large bowl beat the eggs, sugar, and vanilla with an electric mixer until the mixture is very pale and three times the original volume, about 8 minutes.

3. Sift the flour onto the egg mixture little by little, gently folding in each addition. Fold in the butter a little at a time.

4. Spread the batter on the baking sheet. Bake for 25 minutes or until a toothpick inserted in the middle of the cake comes out clean. Let cool completely.

For the mashed strawberries:
5. Meanwhile, in a bowl stir the strawberries with the sugar to coat. Scrape the vanilla seeds over the strawberries and stir well. Set aside for at least 1 hour.

6. Working over a bowl to catch the juices, press the strawberries in a sieve to extract the maximum amount of juice. Mash the strawberries in a mortar and pestle until reduced to a lumpy mixture.

For the sweet cream cheese:
7. Whip the softened cream cheese, icing sugar, and cream into soft mounds.

8. Using a 4-inch (10 cm) cookie cutter, cut out 8 rounds of génoise.

9. Place a round of génoise on each serving plate. Cover them with some of the mashed strawberries, and top with some of the sweet cream cheese. Place another round of génoise on top of each serving, and cover with more mashed strawberries and more sweet cream cheese. Spread sweet cream cheese all around the sides of the cakes, using a spatula to keep it nice and smooth. Garnish with the fresh strawberries and drizzle the strawberry juice all around the cake.

NOTE
Dunk your spatula in hot water before using it to spread the cream cheese. It makes the job a whole lot easier.

PECAN PIE

Prep: 10 min -- Cook: 40 min -- Serves: 8

Mom's famous pie that started it all.

> - **1 cup (250 mL) light brown sugar**
> - **2 tbsp (30 mL) flour**
> - **2 eggs**
> - **½ cup (125 mL) maple syrup**
> - **½ cup (125 mL) 35% cream**
> - **1 (9-inch/23 cm) unbaked pie shell, store-bought or homemade**
> - **1 cup (250 mL) pecans, toasted**

1. Preheat the oven to 350°F (180°C).

2. Whisk together the sugar and flour in a small bowl.

3. In a large bowl, beat the eggs. Stir in the maple syrup and cream. Add the sugar mixture and stir to combine. Pour the filling into the pie shell. Arrange the pecans on top.

4. Bake for about 40 minutes, until the filling is bubbly, the pecans are a little bit crystallized, and the crust is golden brown. This pie will be wobbly when you take it out of the oven but it will set lightly when cooled. Let cool before cutting.

5. Serve with ice cream.

217

INDEX

218

NET WT

RED ABAL

ATLANTIC ABAL

THANKS

Teamwork is the name of the game in a restaurant! The chef often gets all the kudos, but without a good crew and good serving staff, nothing actually gets done. So first and foremost I want to thank every single person at Garde-Manger, everyone who has ever worked there, from the dishwashers to the manager . . . a heartfelt thank you.

It all started with a dream five years ago . . . our very own restaurant. With very little forethought, an even smaller budget, and an enormous amount of work, we opened an eatery that is truly aligned with our beliefs. However, an eatery without patrons has a very short life. We have forged wonderful friendships and met people from all around the world since we opened. We are lucky to have such a group of loyal regulars . . . thank you.

I also want to thank each and every restaurant where I have worked and learned. I want to thank all my mentors and all the passionate people who influenced, motivated, and inspired me. Thank you to my suppliers, my associates, my friends, and my competitors.

CHUCK HUGHES

CHOK

tap katr

adicPtas
ic twind
Fram nicolas

J ohn

Kate
Plus 8

Nico